THE
CONFIDENT
COMMUNICATOR

THE
CONFIDENT
COMMUNICATOR

MASTER
COMMUNICATION SKILLS FOR
PROFESSIONAL SUCCESS

KIM ZOLLER
KERRY PRESTON

JAICO PUBLISHING HOUSE

Ahmedabad Bangalore Bhopal Bhubaneswar Chennai
Delhi Hyderabad Kolkata Lucknow Mumbai

Published by Jaico Publishing House
A-2 Jash Chambers, 7-A Sir Phirozshah Mehta Road
Fort, Mumbai - 400 001
jaicopub@jaicobooks.com
www.jaicobooks.com

Original English language edition published by
The Career Press, Inc.
12 Parish Drive, Wayne
NJ 07470, USA
All right reserved

THE CONFIDENT COMMUNICATOR
ISBN 978-81-8495-882-9

First Jaico Impression: 2017

Printed by
Snehesh Printers
320-A, Shah & Nahar Ind. Est. A-1
Lower Parel, Mumbai - 400 013

Acknowledgments

We started this book many years ago with the simple goal of offering something that wasn't on the market. We wanted to provide a quick and easy reference guide for a business community that didn't have time to read an in-depth etiquette book.

Many thanks to our wonderful clients and seminar participants for asking valid questions. Through their active participation, this book was written with them and their colleagues in mind.

We want to thank our team for their input and excitement regarding this project. We have an amazing support team and could not have accomplished this without them.

We thank the creativity of Andrew Grossman and Roger Pennwill for their wonderful cartoons.

We thank and acknowledge Ben and Sam Zoller and Tim, Luke, Wes, and Nate Reinagel, all of whom gave us many hours of quiet to let us complete this book. We also thank our parents for all of their support through the years.

Contents

Introduction

There is no accomplishment so easy to acquire as politeness, and none more profitable.

—George Bernard Shaw

Successful people leave nothing undone. To them, every detail matters. In many instances, success is determined by interpersonal skills rather than technical skills. After analyzing the records of 10,000 people, the Carnegie Institute of Technology concluded that only 15 percent of job success is due to technical training, intellect, and job skills, and 85 percent of job success is due to personality factors. In other words, job success is determined, in greatest measure, by one's ability to effectively work with other people.

Harvard University's Bureau of Vocational Guidance conducted a study of thousands of men and women who had been fired. The study showed that for every one person who lost a job for failure to do work, two people lost jobs for failure to successfully deal with other people.

Setting yourself apart in today's highly competitive business environment takes thought and planning. To be a truly professional and successful individual in the workplace, not only must you have excellent job skills, but you must have excellent people skills as well.

There is nothing worse than walking into a situation and not knowing how it should be handled. Professionalism is expected and respected. Lack of professionalism can ruin your career. *The Confident Communicator* is about making sure that your mistakes do not get in the way of your career. Nothing goes unnoticed. Don't bring your career to a halt without even realizing it. Walk into every situation feeling confident. Don't ever be in a situation in which you are recounting an interaction and have someone say, "You did *what*?!"

Big Blunder 1 \ Forgetting to Stay One / Step Ahead

Behavior is a mirror in which everyone displays his own image.

—Johann Wolfgang von Goethe

Impressions are made in seconds. Most of the time, these impressions determine the outcome of a situation before the actual interaction begins. We've all heard the saying, "You don't get a second chance to make a first impression." People tend to focus on small things that can affect your future.

Research has confirmed the importance of first impressions. Most businesspeople determine if they want to do business with you based on these first impressions. By planning ahead, you can decide what you want your image to be and what impressions you would like to leave others with. This gives them every opportunity to do business with you, hire you, and be loyal to you.

In an ideal world, others would not judge us. In the professional world, judgments are made and impressions happen within seconds of first meeting someone. It is important to take time to think about first impressions and how others perceive us. Some aspects of first impressions include posture, body language, appearance, and your personal style. If done right, this can play a role in forming favorable impressions that will go a long way toward building your career.

There are three basic components that contribute to a others impression of us:

> The words we use make up 7 percent of an impression.

> The way we sound, that is, our intonation and enunciation make up 38 percent of an impression.

> Our nonverbal messages and our body language make up 55 percent of an impression.

These components determine how others perceive us and how they react to us. Being one step ahead means leaving nothing to chance. You must perfect the details of how you present yourself. Think about the people you know who are successful and professional.

Ask Yourself These Crucial Questions

➡ What makes the people I admire professional?

➡ What did I learn from them that can help me become more professional?

➡ How do I want people to perceive me?

➡ What image do I want to project?

On the Side

"Recently, we were selecting a vendor to furnish our new office. We couldn't believe the treatment we received. Some vendors acted as though they were doing us a favor. Others arrived a few minutes late to our first meeting. We hired the vendor who had the most professional people—the people who treated us well and acted as though they were thrilled to be with us. They were willing to do whatever it took to make us happy. It's a pity that the other vendors overlooked the possibilities. It turned out to be $100,000 worth of business."

—a San Francisco law firm

Tips

Your goal in business should be to give people the opportunity to know how good you are at what you do and actually hear what you have to say. You lose your competitive advantage when people become distracted by aspects of your appearance or by behaviors that you can easily change. Take a look at the first set of tips, which we will expand on throughout this book:

> - Always stay one step ahead of your competition.
> - Keep your emotions in check.
> - Be completely present, no matter the circumstances.
> - Eliminate distractions, including your phone, when engaged in a conversation.
> - Be on time. Even better, be five minutes early to be safe.
> - Be dressed appropriately.
> - Be dressed for where you *want* to be in your career, not for your current position.
> - Be informed.
> - Be protective of your brand on social media.

> ⊳ Be interested, not interesting.

> ⊳ Use appropriate language.

> ⊳ Return telephone calls and emails. You never know when you will need the sender to return a call or note to you.

> ⊳ Be personable, not personal.

> ⊳ Respond yes or no, verbally or in written form, when you are invited to a function. People remember.

> ⊳ Follow up and follow through.

> ⊳ It is better to under-promise and over-deliver.

> ⊳ Send handwritten thank-you notes. (For more information, see Chapter 3.)

> ⊳ Be aware of the messages you are sending all day, every day.

As you continue to advance in your career, be open to opportunities. Adopt a mindset of growth, and always find people to give you feedback for your growth.

Attitude is everything! As Norman Vincent Peale once said, "Any fact facing us is not as important as our attitude toward it, for that determines our success or failure."

Big Blunder 2 \ Using Body Language Improperly

What you are shouts so loud in my ears, I cannot hear what you say.

—Ralph Waldo Emerson

Interesting Study

Amy Cuddy, social psychologist and associate professor at Harvard Business School, shows us the importance of "power posing" to convey confidence, power, and competence. Her research shows how "faking" body postures for just a few minutes changes our cortisol and testosterone levels, helps us perform better in job interviews, and allows us to take risks and handle stressful situations.

The research indicates when individuals feel personally powerful, they are more present and in touch with their own feelings and thoughts. This helps them to connect with the feelings and thoughts of others. With this personal power comes self-motivation and a personal drive to succeed.[1]

If we are both listening to someone's words and watching his or her body language, we always respond to the body language first. Body language accounts for an astounding 55% of an impression, and those impressions are made within seconds. While the meaning behind body language may not be entirely clear, being aware of and understanding the general guidelines regarding body language will provide you with powerful ammunition to convey the nonverbal messages you wish to send.

We all send off "engagement signals"—signals that tell people how confident we feel, how much we want to be there, and how interested we are in them—the moment we come into contact. Whether you are walking down a hallway or arriving at a meeting, be aware of the signals you are sending out and manage them accordingly to make your intended impression.

On the Side

"I was having a terrible experience buying a car. No one was taking me seriously, which was very frustrating. A friend of mine referred me to a dealership where he had been treated well. I decided this was the last place I would visit before I resorted to the Internet. When I walked in, an extremely professional and polished gentleman in a suit came up and greeted me. He made confident eye contact, smiled, put out his hand, introduced himself by name, and welcomed me to the dealership. I was sold! The salespeople at the two top-notch dealerships I visited previously had given me fishy handshakes and made no eye contact. It was as though they were saying that they didn't want my business."

—Female advertising agency executive

During the next week, be aware of your own body language, and observe the body language and gestures of the people around you—while on the telephone, in a meeting, on an elevator, or while driving or dining.

Ask Yourself These Crucial Questions

- How does my body language relate to how I feel?
- Has my awareness changed my body language at all?
- What did I notice about others?
- What perceptions do I have and what impressions have I formed?

Tips

Handshakes

- Your handshake must be firm. A firm handshake communicates confidence.
- The web between your thumb and forefinger should meet the web of the other person's hand.
- Extend your hand immediately at the beginning and end of an interaction.
- Stand when you are shaking hands.
- Make direct eye contact and smile while shaking hands.
- Smiling while shaking someone's hand builds a connection.
- If you realize that you "missed hands" and the handshake was not good,

Interesting Study

Greg Stewart, associate professor of management and organizations at the University of Iowa, has conducted numerous studies on handshakes and their effects. "We've always heard that interviewers make up their mind about a person in the first two or three minutes of an interview, no matter how long the interview lasts. We found that the first impression begins with a handshake that sets the tone for the rest of the interview.... We probably don't consciously remember a person's handshake or whether it was good or bad," Stewart says. "But the handshake is one of the first nonverbal clues we get about the person's overall personality, and that impression is what we remember."[2]

make a comment like, "Oh, that wasn't a very good handshake; can we do that again?" It is better to do that than leave the other person feeling negative about the impression you made.

» Keep your body leaning forward. Do not lean back or put a shoulder back. This gives an impression of arrogance.

Eye Contact

Eye communication involves more extended eye contact—at least three to five seconds. It establishes rapport, helps others retain what you are saying, increases your persuasiveness, and drives involvement.

» Make eye contact immediately when meeting a person.

» Maintain eye contact throughout your conversation.

» Do not dart your eyes from one place to the next, even if you are nervous.

» When you ask or answer a question, make and maintain eye contact.

» When you shake hands at the end of the interaction, maintain eye contact.

» Positive eye contact does not mean staring. Make eye contact during approximately 85 percent of the conversation.

» Do not roll your eyes when you do not agree with what is being said.

» Do not hold an "eye communication sidebar" with another person regarding something being said by another person in the conversation.

» Do not squint to show annoyance. Keep eyes open and engaged.

» Long slow blinks or keeping your eyes closed while speaking is distracting to others.

➧ Use your eye contact to build rapport. Validate, acknowledge, show agreement, and encourage through your eye contact. Keeping your eyes wide and nodding your head "yes" reflects your positive feelings.

Facial Expressions

Basic facial expressions that depict human emotions of happiness, sadness, fear, disgust, surprise, and anger are recognized around the world, with minor variations. In 1872, Charles Darwin published these findings in *The Expressions of the Emotions in Man and Animals*.

Smile

> ⊳ If you do not smile a lot, practice, practice, and practice smiling more. Practice in a mirror to get used to the feeling.

> ⊳ A smile creates rapport and makes you and others feel good.

> ⊳ Smiles correlate to health, happiness, and success.

> ⊳ Studies have shown that the brain cannot tell the difference between a fake smile and a real smile. If you don't feel it, fake it!

Interesting Study

A study by psychologist Dr. Robert Zajonc suggests that if you put a smile on your face, it can move you in the direction of a positive feeling. The research points to a cause-and-effect relationship between brain activities like smiling and happiness.[3] Your movements can send powerful messages.

Posture

➧ Do not slouch when sitting or standing. This type of posture is often associated with a lack of confidence.

» Use your upright posture as a way to show that you know what you are talking about and are sure of yourself.

» Use your breath to help you keep an upright posture during difficult conversations.

» Keep in mind that all the studies on body language show that bad posture not only sends negative impressions out to other people, but it also affects how you feel about yourself.

Strategies to Improve Your Posture

▷ Pull your shoulders back and lift your chin up slightly.

▷ Balance on both feet.

▷ While seated, make sure the curve in your lower back is away from the chair while lengthening your torso.

▷ Breath deeply. Shallow breaths make you slouch.

Arm and Hand Positions

» Do not put your hands in your pockets.

» Keep your hands in view, either on your lap or at your side.

» Keep your fingers and nails out of your mouth and preferably away from your face.

» Do not cross your arms. This behavior is often misinterpreted as anger, lack of interest, or boredom.

» Do not fidget with your pens, hair, rings, and so forth.

» Do not point your fingers or make a fist. These actions may make others feel intimidated.

» Always cover your mouth when coughing or yawning. When coughing try to cough into your forearm. This alleviates others from focusing on the germs that you may transfer through your handshakes or touching pens, and so on.

» Keep your arm gestures open, and maintain open palms.

Overall Body Movement that Portrays Confidence

▶ Walk through your office with your head up straight and eyes focused in front of you; smile at people you pass and take confident strides.

▶ You may move quickly, but try not to look as though you are frazzled or in a hurry.

▶ Keep your lower body still while sitting in a meeting.

▶ Fidgeting is a sign of anxiety. Still hands with purposeful movement portray confidence.

Remember that people focus on your body language even before you begin to speak, and 55 percent of the impression you make is nonverbal. How people initially perceive you sets the stage for all the interactions that follow. A negative impression can be damaging to your image and is very hard to overcome.

Even if you don't feel confident in a situation, others must think you are! Make sure the signals you send are positive ones.

Big Blunder 3

Being Sloppy With Written and Verbal Correspondence

Simple speech is the best and truest eloquence.

—Ralph Waldo Emerson

Positive personal interactions allow you to build a rapport with others that will guarantee your success. Knowing when to write a note or make a phone call is priceless. Time is limited, but if you don't take the time when the time is right, you will waste more of it later. Success in building relationships is in the details.

Ask Yourself These Crucial Questions

» When was the last time a vendor or salesperson wrote me a note to say thank you?

On the Side

"Recently, we met with a prospective client. We noticed a bulletin board at the side of his desk that had a variety of little note cards on it. Noticing that we were looking at it, our client said, 'Everything being equal, I do business with vendors who send me notes thanking me for my time and my business.' Handwritten notes do make a difference!"

—Image Dynamics executives

22

➧ Did it make an impression on me?

➧ If I could get my desired result by taking five minutes to do something, would I?

Written Correspondence

It is acceptable to put a business card in a handwritten note only when the recipient has asked for a card and is expecting one. When you include a business card that has not been asked for, you make a very personal touch impersonal. This can damage the rapport you are trying to build.

When writing a handwritten note, use folding notepaper or note cards that measure at least 3 1/2 by 5 inches. These are known as informal notes. Plain white or cream-colored informal notes are available at all stationery stores. Stationery that is engraved, thermographed, embossed, or printed adds a personal touch.

Types of written correspondence include personal letters, condolence letters, letters of congratulations, thank-you notes, reference letters, letters of introduction, and letters of greeting.

Handwritten notes should be written:

> when someone takes the time to meet with you;

> following any type of interview—internal or external;

> when you have been a guest at a cocktail or dinner party;

> when you have been invited to someone's home;

> when you receive a gift;

> when customers or associates have been promoted;

> when customers or associates have had a death in their family; and

> when customers or associates celebrate a marriage, the birth or adoption of a child, or receive some special recognition.

Remember, to be an effective writer you should:

> ⟩ have a strong sense of purpose about a letter before writing it;

> ⟩ limit your letter to one page;

> ⟩ get to the point early (within the first two sentences);

> ⟩ emphasize the reader's perspective (ask yourself how your message will benefit him or her);

> ⟩ never write in anger;

> ⟩ be personable and not use a form letter, as it may not fully apply; and

> ⟩ end with an action item that suggests the next step.

Note Writing Do's and Don'ts

▶ Do send a note in the mail.

▶ Do not email a thank-you note. If time is of the essence, you can send an email immediately, but always follow-up with a handwritten note.

▶ Do write a note within three days of meeting, preferably. If you forget, write it as soon as you remember; it will always make a positive impression.

▶ Never send a letter with any visible deletions or corrections.

▶ Do handwrite the envelope of a handwritten note.

On the Side

"I interviewed someone recently and at the end of the interview she pulled out a prewritten thank-you note. While the gesture was nice, the point of the note is to have the interviewer remember you a day or two after the interview is over. You do this by mentioning something specific that happened during the interview."

—Joyce B, partner at law firm

Examples of Written Correspondence

A "Nice to Meet You" Note

Dear John,

It was so nice meeting you yesterday. I appreciate you taking the time; I know you are extremely busy. Your work sounds so interesting. I would love to hear more about it. I look forward to seeing you at the next Association meeting.

Sincerely yours,

Kim Zoller

A Thank-You Note

Dear Matt,

Thank you for giving me the opportunity to work with you. I know you have a choice of where you purchase your printing and I appreciate you choosing us. Please do not hesitate to call if you need anything or have any questions. I will follow up with you in a couple of weeks.

All the best,

Kerry Preston

An Internal Interview Note

Dear Mike,

As you know, I really enjoy working here and I appreciate you considering me for the opening in your department. Every new challenge is exciting, and I am looking forward to the opportunity.

I will follow up with you next week as you suggested. Thank you again for considering me.

Sincerely,

John Smith

An External Interview Note

Dear Mike,

It was a pleasure meeting you to discuss the sales position. I have such a high regard for [name of company] and I look forward to the opportunity to work with you and your team. Thank you for considering me.

I will follow up with you next week as you suggested.

Sincerely yours,

Mary Smith

A "Thanks for Having Me Over" Note

Dear Jane,

What a wonderful evening! Thank you for inviting me to your holiday party. I enjoyed meeting everyone and spending some time with you. I look forward to seeing you soon.

Warmest regards,

Kerry Preston

A Condolences Note

Dear Susan,

I was so sorry to hear about your mother. This must be a difficult time for you. I want you to know that you and your family are in my thoughts.

With deepest sympathy,

Kim Zoller

Verbal Correspondence

It's not only what you say, but how you say it. Technology will never take the place of a live voice. Make the most of every opportunity you have to connect with people. These connections help you build your professional reputation.

Verbal Correspondence Do's and Don'ts

▶ Put a smile in your voice and on your face when appropriate.

▶ Block out all background noise, such as music, pets, eating, and so on.

▶ Make a call only when you have the time.

▶ Do not put the other person on hold.

▶ Stay focused and engaged. People can tell when you are doing something else, like typing an email, while talking to them.

Examples of Verbal Correspondence
An Introductory Phone Call

Introductory telephone calls should always start with:

"Susan, this is [your name] with [company name]. Do you have a moment?" Or, "Susan, this is [your name] with [company name]. [Referral source] suggested that I give you a call. Do you have a moment?"

If someone you call says he or she is busy and will return your call later, respond by saying,

"If I don't hear from you by Wednesday, may I call you back? Thank you." Suggest a time within the next couple of days. People get busy, so put yourself in charge of the situation.

A Verbal Condolence

"Susan, hello, it's John Smith. I don't want to take too much of your time; I just want you to know how sorry I am to hear about your mother. Please call me if you need anything."

A Verbal Thank-You

"Susan, hi, it's Kim Zoller. Thank you so much for your help on the project. I appreciate your time and help. Please let me know when I can return the favor."

A Verbal Acknowledgment
> "Susan, hi, it's Kerry Preston. I was thinking about you today and wanted to wish you a happy birthday. Have a wonderful day."

Responding to an Invitation Marked RSVP

The rules for RSVPs pertain to both business and social functions (that is, meetings, seminars, after-hour parties, etc.). When an invitation asks for an RSVP, you must send a reply either in writing or verbally. It doesn't matter whether you are accepting or declining the invitation. Some invitations may state something to the effect of "RSVP only if declining." In these cases, you should respond only if you cannot attend.

RSVP Do's and Don'ts

- A verbal or written response should be made within one week if an RSVP is requested.

- The RSVP should be made by phone if a telephone number is included with the invitation.

- Once you have made your RSVP, the host must be made aware of any changes as soon as possible.

- Do not send someone in your place if you are unable to attend.

- Do not bring a guest unless the invitation is addressed specifically to you and a guest.

If you fail to RSVP or you respond yes and do not attend, you can be sure that your host will remember! Negative impressions are difficult to overcome and can be extremely costly in the long run.

Both written and verbal correspondences are crucial in cultivating relationships and gaining a competitive advantage. They should be looked at as opportunities for you to make favorable impressions and to help you stay one step ahead of the competition.

Big Blunder 4 〉 Breaking the Rules for Introductions

Civility costs nothing and buys everything.

—Lady Mary Wortley Montagu

Knowing the whos and whens of introductions is a key component in maintaining your competitive advantage. Many people draw blanks or forget names when they are trying to make introductions. There are many reasons for this, but often in a business setting it is because they feel overwhelmed with the responsibility of leading the introduction process.

Ask Yourself These Crucial Questions

- Have I ever been in a situation in which someone did not extend his or her hand for a handshake when we first met? Did it make me feel uncomfortable?
- Do I introduce myself by name and with a handshake when I first meet a business acquaintance?
- Do I introduce the others around me?

On the Side

"It was a Sunday and I went to the mall. Dressed in jeans and a T-shirt, I did not look the way I look during the week. I saw a client with whom I had a good relationship but had not seen in years. I walked up to her with a big smile on my face and said, 'Hi. How are you?' She smiled and gave me a big hug. As she stepped back from the hug, she looked at me apologetically and said, 'I'm so sorry. Please tell me your name again.' From that moment on, I decided that it is best to introduce myself in any situation where someone may not be able to remember me, what we did together, or my name."

—New Jersey sales representative

If there is the slightest chance that someone may not be able to remember your name or how he or she knows you, make it a policy to put out your hand and introduce yourself immediately. This will put the other person at ease right away.

Introductions are important. Always remember to introduce yourself and others in your group. When you introduce yourself, make sure you state your full name and your company name (for example, "Hello. I'm Kim Zoller with Image Dynamics. Nice to meet you."). If there are others in your group, introduce them as well (for example, "This is Joann Smith and John Wise. They are also with Image Dynamics.").

In most instances when making introductions, you should mention the most important person first, that is, the person to whom you want to show greatest respect or honor. Phrases like "I'd like you to meet . . . ," "Have you met . . . ," and "This is . . . ," may be helpful. It is all right to mention the least important person first if you phrase your introduction to prioritize the person of note, such as, "[Name of person], I'd like to introduce you to [name of important person]."

Examples

"Susan, I'd like to introduce you to my manager, Joe. Joe, this is my wife."

"Joe, I'd like to introduce you to Kerry, with [company name]. Kerry, Joe is my manager."

Tips

» In business, gender is irrelevant. Introduce the most important person first, showing the greater respect to him or her.

» Wait until the introduction is complete before you shake hands.

» Listen closely to hear the other person's name so you can use it in the conversation. Try and use it a few times throughout the conversation if appropriate.

» Introduce yourself if you do not remember the person's name and think they may not remember yours either.

» Do not give yourself a title or state what you do in an introduction.

» Do not hand out business cards during introductions.

Examples

Introducing Someone to Your Boss

"John, I'd like you to meet my wife, Susan. Susan, John is my boss."

Introducing Someone to Your Customer

"Kerry, have you met my manager, Joe? Joe, Kerry works with [company name]."

Introducing Several People to Your Customer

"Lisa, this is our accounting department. Everyone, Lisa is with [company name]."

Big Blunder 5 ⟩ Making Small Talk and Networking Inappropriately

Talk to a man about himself and he will listen for hours.

—Benjamin Disraeli

Knowing how to network and make appropriate small talk can open doors that determine lifetime success. If you are not networking today, you may be missing some wonderful opportunities. Be prepared with the proper protocol for any situation in which you may meet someone or make a contact that could be beneficial to you. Stay on your toes so you do not lose any opportunities.

Bob couldn't figure out why his phone never rang after handing out 1,000 business cards in two days.

Ask Yourself These Crucial Questions

» What topics are appropriate when conversing during networking situations?

» Do I know what I want to achieve at every networking event?

» While I am making small talk with someone, do I know what I am trying to get out of the interaction?

Networking and Small-Talk Specifics

Most people are uncomfortable making small talk. You should always prepare for small talk and networking opportunities ahead of time. Having a plan in mind before you go out will make the situation easier for you. The following "Small-Talk Don'ts" will keep you from offending someone. We've included some "Small-Talk Do's" as well. These small-talk tips can be used in all business situations. They will help you initiate conversations and open doors of opportunity.

On the Side

"As I am writing this, I am sitting on an airplane. The person sitting next to me just happens to be someone who makes decisions for his company about training. It reminds me of another time I was sitting on an airplane, tired and desperate to get home. I did not want to talk to anyone. I was sitting next to a lady who asked me what I did for a living. Luckily, I put a smile on my face and answered her cordially. Before I knew it, she was telling me that she was a top executive for a Fortune 100 company. Based on that networking opportunity, my company is now doing a lot of work for her and her team."

—Corporate trainer

> Do your research and be prepared to hold a conversation using that information. Take time to learn about the person and the company.

> Plan three items or stories to share.

> ⊳ Prepare four generic questions to ask. Make sure they are open-ended questions that cannot be answered with a simple yes or no.

> ⊳ Use the newspaper, an experience, current events, or books and movies as subjects.

> ⊳ Think about each item or issue carefully. Consider the ramifications a topic might have, questions it might generate, or opinions that others might have on it.

Small-Talk Taboos

⊳ Politics	⊳ Religion
⊳ Sexism	⊳ Racist or ethnocentric comments
⊳ Sexual orientation	⊳ Salary
⊳ Gossip	⊳ Negativism
⊳ Private matters	

A discussion may center on something that is of little or no consequence to you, but the topic may be of great importance to the person with whom you are having the discussion. Always keep in mind that not all people think or feel as you do!

Small-Talk Don'ts

⊳ Giving too much personal information	⊳ Giving an overabundance of detail
⊳ Monopolizing the conversation	⊳ Relationship therapy and sharing too much personal information
⊳ Discussing children too much	⊳ Interrogating rather than conversing
⊳ Interrupting the other person	⊳ Complaining
⊳ Trying to one-up the other person	⊳ Glancing around the room while someone is conversing with you

Small-Talk Safe Topics

▷ Career background	▷ Achievements and goals
▷ Upcoming events	▷ Community involvement
▷ Entertainment, such as favorite movies and books	▷ Current events, as long as they are not controversial
▷ Current location	▷ Seasonal topics
▷ Hobbies and leisure activities	▷ Family (if the other person brings it up first, but don't get too personal)

Small-Talk Do's

▷ Shake hands firmly and introduce yourself	▷ Be aware of the other person's time
▷ Keep a positive attitude	▷ Smile
▷ Thank the person for the conversation when finished	▷ Ask leading questions from what the person is enjoying discussing
▷ Listen carefully, this will give you more to discuss	

Ready. . . Set. . . Talk

"Hi. I'm Kim Zoller with Image Dynamics. It's nice to meet you. This looks like an interesting meeting. How long have you been involved in the association?"
Don't continue speaking. Listen to the response to your question.
"How did you get started in your business?"
Don't continue speaking. Listen to the response to your question.
"What do you enjoy most about what you do?"
Don't continue speaking. Listen to the response to your question.
"What significant changes have you seen in your industry through the years?"
Don't continue speaking. Listen to the response to your question.

"What do you see as upcoming trends?"
Don't continue speaking. Listen to the response to your question.

Tips

» Take a deep breath and relax. Figure out what your body is saying.

» Wear your name tag on your *right* lapel.

» Hold your drink or food in your left hand so you can shake with your right hand.

» Use a mint if you need one. Do not chew gum.

» Hand out business cards only when you are specifically asked for them. Ask for a business card in return and follow up.

» Ask for a business card at the end of the conversation if no one has requested one of yours.

» Make eye contact before you start the conversation.

» Extend your hand and introduce yourself, giving your full name (and your company name when applicable).

» Ask questions. Be interested, not interesting. If someone thinks that you are only interested in talking about yourself, you will come across as conceited and disinterested in anyone else. You will also seem less interesting than you really are!

» Use the person's name throughout the conversation, but be careful not to overuse it.

» Be careful when you compliment another person. Compliment someone only if you sincerely feel that way.

» Wait to see if the other person brings up personal issues before you start talking about them.

» Never discuss personal problems. Negativity is always a reflection of your personality.

» Talk about a relevant article you have read recently or a seminar you have attended that you feel might enhance the conversation.

» Keep abreast of world events.

» Keep a log of all of the contacts you have made.

» Keep track of all of your discussions and any other pertinent information (that is, what you were wearing, specifics about each of the people you met, family, hobbies, and so on).

Creating a Lasting Impression

» You may not be remembered for good manners, but it is a certainty that you will be remembered for bad manners.

» Gather business cards and follow up.

» Send a handwritten "Nice to Meet You" note.

» Never promise something that you cannot deliver. People will remember forever.

» If you see an article about someone you know or have met, cut out the article and send it to that person with a note. You would be amazed at what an impression this makes!

» The world is a very small place. Once you have burned a bridge, you may have burned many. News travels fast, and your reputation is all you have.

Networking and Socializing Over Meals

Many deals are sealed at the dining table. If you are not comfortable doing business over a meal, you may be losing out on a great number of business opportunities. Business dining is about business. When you are eating a business meal, remember that you are there to build rapport and build your relationships.

Hosting

> Ask the person(s) what type of food they would like.

> If you are partial to a particular cuisine, make sure that your guest likes it as well.

> When you do the inviting, you are the host and you should pay the bill. Vendors are the one exception to this rule: they usually pay the bill.

> Let your guests order first.

> Do not start eating until everyone has their food.

Being a Guest

> Do not start eating until the host starts or gives you the go ahead.

> Do not order the most expensive item or wine on the menu.

Handling the Check

> When you are the host, arrange beforehand for the check to be given to you.

> Do not argue about paying the bill if the other person insists on paying. If you feel that you should be the one paying the bill, suggest that the other person get it the next time.

Seating Arrangements

If hosting, allow your guests to face out or face the better view. There are two basic reasons for doing this: first, it is just

> **On the Side**
>
> "I was sitting with one of my best clients, the general manager of a top Fortune 500 company. He spends a great deal of his time entertaining clients and networking. He ordered a steak and proceeded to stab the piece of steak with his fork and saw away with his knife. I know what *I* was thinking, so I can imagine what his clients or colleagues think when they dine together."
>
> —Operations manager

more polite; and second, it is better to have your guest be distracted by a passerby than for you to be distracted. If you are looking at everything but your guests, they may think that you are not interested in them. Never take the chance that your behavior might be interpreted in the wrong way.

Place Setting

When you first sit down to dine, the table may be filled with glasses, silverware, and plates of all different shapes and sizes. If you are at all confused, think of a BMW automobile. The letters BMW are read from left to right. Read your place setting in the same way—starting at the left and moving to the right. Think of the letter B as standing for your bread plate, which is located on your left. The letter M stands for your meal plate (or your entrée plate) and is located in the center. The letter W stands for your water glass and all other glasses or cups for liquids. These are located on your right just above the knives, spoons, and cocktail fork.

Bad Ideas for Ordering

  ⟩ Long pasta, such as linguini or spaghetti, if you do not know how to eat it properly.

  ⟩ Carbonated drinks

Body Language while Networking

Actions speak louder than words. Sound familiar? Make sure your body language sends a message about how happy you are to be there.

▶ Stand confidently and extend your hand immediately when meeting or greeting someone.

▶ Eye contact must be maintained while shaking hands and talking to someone. Don't worry about what others are doing. Stay focused.

➧ Your posture must be erect and confident. If you slouch, you send others the message that you lack confidence, that you are not friendly, or that you are unapproachable.

➧ Keep your arms uncrossed, even if you are more comfortable crossing them. Crossed arms may send a message of boredom or defensiveness.

Kissing, Hugging, and Touching

➧ Cultural differences dictate the norm. Learn the differences and behave accordingly.

➧ Take the lead from your client or associate, as long as he or she stays professional.

➧ If you are uncomfortable with the cultural norm, fake it. Build rapport, don't break it.

Big Blunder 6 〉 Forgetting Names

*Who steals my purse steals trash. . . . But he that filches
from me my good name robs me of that which not
enriches him and makes me poor indeed.*

—William Shakespeare, *Othello*

Remembering someone's name is one of the most powerful tools for networking and building relationships. There is nothing greater than the sound of one's own name. Normally, people are so focused on what they are going to say when they meet someone, they either don't hear that person's name or they just don't remember it. Many people are offended and take it very personally when their name is not remembered. The first or second time you forget someone's name, you should apologize and ask for his or her name again. If it is still a problem for you, make sure you get the person's name from someone else.

Remembering names does matter!

On the Side

"Every month, I go to a vendor breakfast. It never seems to fail that I run into Joe, the one person who never remembers my name. Joe does business with my company and he has had to deal with me. Recently, I was promoted to manager of training and development. In my new position, I am responsible for making decisions about which vendors the company uses. I have decided to look for someone other than Joe who can do what he does. It's amazing how his lack of interest in me has made me want to look for someone else."

—UPS executive

Ask Yourself These Crucial Questions

» How do I feel when someone remembers my name?

» Am I uncomfortable when I forget another person's name?

» When people remember my name at a meeting, event, or workshop, am I more inclined to think about doing business with them?

Tips

» If at an event with someone you know, ask that person to remind you of names you have forgotten.

» If you cannot recall someone's name, own up to it and ask for his or her name again. If you have asked multiple times, do not ask again; it is insulting if the person has told you more than two times.

» When you are being introduced, focus on the other person's name, not on what you want to say after the introduction.

» Repeat the person's name immediately (for example, "John, it is so nice to meet you.").

» Visualize the name (for example, try to see it written across the person's forehead).

➤ Use the person's name throughout the conversation. Be careful you don't repeat it so often that it becomes awkward.

➤ Try to associate this person's name with an object or another person with the same name (for example, you might associate Justin Allen with Justin Bieber, Ronald Smith with Ronald Regan, Mr. Campbell with Campbell's Soup, and so on).

➤ When people express interest in talking to you again, add them to your phone on the spot.

➤ Write down something you learned about people you met so that you can recall it when you speak to them again. This also helps you remember them for the next time you see them.

Many of the previous strategies for remembering are not easy to learn. However, with time, practice, and awareness, you will be able to use them effectively. The ability to remember names is a powerful tool. It will help you in your quest to increase your competitive advantage.

Big Blunder 7 \ Lacking Technology Etiquette

Email is a unique communication vehicle for a lot of reasons. However, email is not a substitute for direct interaction.

—Bill Gates

In every seminar, we ask people to tell us what offends them at work. Lately, the majority of stories have involved technology (problems with emails, voicemails, and so on). These updated modes of communication have become informal ways for us to keep in touch with one another and to help get our messages across quickly. Despite the fact that technology has changed the way people look at communication, it has not changed the way people react to the messages they receive.

In today's hectic business environments, time has become an expensive commodity. Time-saving tools such as email and voicemail increase the speed of our communications. These technologies are a less formal mode for communication, but it is important to remember that your effectiveness can be lost if you are too informal. Keep in mind that you are always creating an impression whenever and however you communicate. Always make sure that the impressions you are making are positive ones!

Some of these modes of communication tend to be used more often than others, such as emailing over faxing. It is still important that we maintain our professional impact by communicating in the most professional manner through any mode.

On the Side

"Recently, a client told us that someone was asked to leave his company because he had sent an extremely vulgar joke to everyone on his email list by mistake. Unfortunately, the list included customers and the CEO of the company. Another client told us how someone had sent a message to a coworker that read, 'I NEED TO SEE YOU IN MY OFFICE.' The sender of the message wanted to brainstorm about a meeting he was supposed to have later that day. However, the recipient assumed the sender was furious and was going to reprimand him. It took an entire day for the situation to be resolved and for feelings to be soothed. What a waste of valuable time!"

—Image Dynamics trainer

Ask Yourself These Crucial Questions

● What message am I trying to send?

● What is offensive to me? (Often, the things that offend you are likely to offend others.)

● Is the recipient going to understand the meaning of my message?

Tips

If you are leaving a message or writing an email that you think may be misconstrued, have someone read the message or listen to it and give you feedback before you send it.

Email

▶ If you have something pertinent to say or need closure immediately, it is preferable to speak with the person face-to-face or call him or her on the telephone.

▶ Do not write anything emotional or that you may want to recant. Reread it three times if you are unsure.

▶ Put questionable emails in your drafts, and go back and reread them an hour later. This may give you a different perspective.

▶ Email does not take the place of a handwritten note.

▶ Check your email every day.

▶ Always check your spelling and grammar, and proofread the text before you send anything.

▶ Put the purpose of the email in the subject line and put the action you want taken in the first sentence or paragraph.

▶ Do not "reply all" unless relevant to all parties.

▶ Keep your email short and to the point.

▶ If the message you are sending has nothing to do with a previous correspondence, don't use the "reply" button. Begin a new email message when addressing a new topic.

▶ Be careful when you use all capital letters in your message. Most messages that are written in all capitals READ AS THOUGH YOU ARE YELLING!

▶ Forwarding emails to everyone in your address book is not a good idea unless you are sure that all of them need to receive that specific message.

▶ Sending emails with jokes to anyone with whom you do business is inappropriate and shows a lack of professionalism.

▶ Give the receiver adequate time to respond.

➧ Know or set your company/department's culture and expectations regarding appropriate email response time no matter what time/day the email was sent. Caveat: as a leader of a company/department, you set the tone and expectation. Keep in mind that, uninterrupted personal time makes people more motivated while at work.

Interesting Study

In a study titled "Hot Buttons and Time Sinks, " researchers William Becker, Marcus Butts, and Wendy Boswell interviewed 341 working adults through Facebook, LinkedIn, and Twitter. They asked a sample of people to track their feelings for seven days about how they feel when receiving and opening a work email when not working or after they had gone home. The surveyed group reported that they were angry and read the messages as negative and requiring a lot of time. The people who were purposefully trying to separate work and personal life felt that this was interfering with their personal lives and affecting their work-life balance.[1]

Voicemail
Outgoing Messages

➧ Use proper English (for example, "Please leave a message for Kim or me," not "Kim or myself").

➧ State your full name and your company name (for example, "You have reached the voicemail of Kim Zoller with Image Dynamics. Please leave your message . . .").

➧ Keep your message short.

➧ If you change your message daily, update it first thing in the morning or last thing in the evening. Don't forget!

Leaving Messages

» Always state your full name and company name.

» Make your point succinctly.

» Leave your phone number slowly at the end of the message, even if the person knows your phone number. You will get a return call 90 percent faster.

» Write your number down as you say it. This will help you say it at an appropriate speed.

» Use clear articulation, enunciation, and pronunciation.

» Speak slowly so that the person on the other end of the message can easily follow what you are saying.

Conference Calls

» Be on time, which is really five minutes early.

» When you arrive on the call, state your name to announce you are on the call.

» State your name before speaking.

» Be prepared and stay focused.

» Have a call facilitator direct the questions if necessary.

» Keep the call succinct.

» Do not speak over others. Apologize and ask permission before interrupting. "Kerry, I'm sorry to interrupt you. May I ask you a question?"

» It is important to have a voice and contribute to conference calls, unless you are only the note-taker.

» Eliminate background noises, especially when putting others on hold.

» Mute the call when you're not speaking.

Cell Phones

» Turn off your phone in all meetings, including seminars and presentations.

» If there is a family emergency, apologize and ask permission to keep your phone on silent mode. When you answer your telephone, politely excuse yourself and take your call away from the meeting.

» While you are in public, be very careful about what you say. Remember that everyone can hear what you are saying.

» Have private conversations in private.

» Do not text or email on your phone during a meeting.

» Do not look at your phone while having a face-to-face conversation.

» Keeping your phone on vibrate is distracting to others. While in a meeting, silence your telephone completely or turn it off.

Texting

» Many of the rules that apply to emails also apply to texting.

» Be careful that you do not use shortcuts or acronyms.

» Think about the receiver and your relationship. Text accordingly.

» Remember that your brand is reflected in every text message. Business is business; don't ruin your brand by being too casual while texting. Stay professional.

» Read your message again and check spelling.

» It is rude to text while having a face-to-face conversation.

» When in a meeting, people know when you're texting. Stay engaged in the meeting.

Faxes

▶ Call or email before you fax to let the receiver know the fax is on the way, or after you fax to confirm that it was received.

▶ Include a cover page or sticky note to let the receiver know who sent the fax, who should receive it, and how many pages there are.

▶ Always let the receiver know exactly how many pages to expect.

▶ Confidential or revealing information should never be faxed to a communal fax machine. Before you send a fax, find out if there are others in the office who will have access to the fax you are sending. If so, you may want to send the information via a more private method of communication.

Webinars

When You Are the Host

> Preparation is critical.

> Introductions should be made by all speakers and, if possible, all attendees.

> Begin and end on time.

> Participants should receive an agenda in advance.

> Speak clearly and articulate fully.

> Record the webinar for future use.

> Engage participants through polls and chat function.

> Captivate participants with strong visuals.

> Clean up your desktop; turn off alerts and chimes if your desktop is shared with participants.

> Distribute materials in advance.

When You Are the Participant

> Announce yourself when asking questions.

> Eliminate background noises. Mute your microphone when not speaking.

> Be on time—and a few minutes early is on time.

> Test your equipment in advance or leave some extra time to join the webinar.

> The person leading the webinar gets a warning when you not participating.

> Be attentive. Give verbal feedback when possible.

> Speak up if you are experiencing a delay or technology is not working properly.

> Speak clearly and articulate fully.

> Ensure you have the proper materials prior to the start of the webinar.

> Use the "raise your hand" icon if you have a question. Be an active participant.

Videoconferencing

> Think of a videoconference as a face-to-face meeting.

> Look at the camera as though the lens is the person to whom you are speaking.

> Watch your posture at all times. Use appropriate posture when sitting or standing.

> Do not whisper to your neighbor. This is rude and will be perceived negatively.

Computers During Meetings

The purpose of many meetings is to build rapport. You accomplish this by making eye contact with others at the meeting. If you feel that you must jot down some notes on your computer, make sure that someone else from your team is making eye contact with others at the meeting. Attend to the following extremely important considerations.

> ᐳ Establish ground rules for participants if you are leading the meeting.

> ᐳ Focus on the people at the meeting, not on your computer screen.

> ᐳ Keep your computer off the table unless you need it.

> ᐳ Remember why you are at the meeting. (For more information, see Chapter 10.)

All Social Media

The following guidelines can help you build your brand and reputation on all of your social media platforms.

▶ Post photographs that you would be comfortable showing anyone, including your parents, children, bosses, colleagues, and clients.

▶ Do not link yourself to behavior that could be seen as inappropriate in a business setting.

▶ Remember that your friends are not the only ones looking at your social media. You may want a job one day that may be affected by something you posted years ago.

▶ Comments should always be appropriate and kind.

Big Blunder 8 ⟩ Cubicle Mayhem

Our personality can dictate what our office or cubicle at work looks like. It's always interesting to walk through a workspace and see what people have put up on their walls. Decorating and personalizing our office space can be fun and a way to express ourselves but may not express how we want to be seen as a professional. A balance is needed between your personal and professional self. We are not suggesting that you remove your personal self. Just remember that others' perceptions of your capabilities are more shaped through nonverbal vehicles. Your office space is just one of those nonverbal vehicles.

Ask Yourself These Crucial Questions

➧ Who will see my office, and do I feel that it represents me well when they see it?

➧ What does it say about me?

➧ Is it distracting? Does it take away from my work?

Decorations

➧ Keep them to a minimum. You don't want them to be overwhelming when people walk into your space.

❧ Make sure photos depict appropriate scenes.

❧ Obey company policies.

❧ Add a small lamp or a plant to personalize your space.

Organization

❧ Keep your work area orderly.

❧ Take time at the end of the day to return things to their correct locations.

❧ Plan time each month to discard papers, magazines, reports, and other materials.

Sound Volume

❧ Be mindful of your voice volume while on the phone or speaking to visitors.

❧ Avoid using the speaker function on your phone when others are around your cubicle.

❧ Use headphones or play music at a very low volume. The volume should be set so that others cannot hear the sound.

❧ Wear earbuds if allowed; just keep the volume low so you can hear your coworkers if necessary. Be mindful not to overuse your earbuds because that makes you seem antisocial and unavailable.

Smells

❧ Avoid wearing too much fragrance.

❧ Avoid air-freshener products and scented candles.

❧ Avoid eating foods that have strong odors in your cubicle.

❧ Place empty food containers in larger disposals away from your desk.

Interruptions

▶ Curb interruptions when you are faced with deadlines or trying to work.

▶ Stand up when someone comes to see you.

▶ Be clear on your time constraints.

▶ Avoid facing out and avoid eye contact with others passing by when trying to get something done.

▶ Eliminate phone and computer alerts.

▶ Set the stage with others by encouraging them to use a calendar to schedule time together.

▶ Let others know that, going forward, in an effort to make the most of everyone's time, rather than welcoming interruptions or drop-ins, you will instead need to set up a time to meet in advance.

Body Language

▶ When talking to someone in your cubicle, face your body toward him or her, not your screen. Be present and engaged.

▶ Your office/cubicle at work, while your domain, is still a place of work. Keep your body language positive, open, and not too relaxed. For example, feet up on your desk is generally inappropriate.

▶ Building relationships with your coworkers happens when you take time to wander around as well as let others into your workspace.

Big Blunder 9 〉 Failing to Follow the Guidelines for Professional Dress

The apparel oft proclaims the man.

—William Shakespeare, *Hamlet*

People assume the outer package reflects the inner person. Our clothes, our accessories, and our general appearance contribute greatly to the impression we give others. Remember, our non-verbal messages account for a full 55% of the total impression others have of us. Professional clothing should be seen as an investment in your future

that adds to your competitive advantage. Every work environment is different. It is important to dress professionally for your particular job while still maintaining your individualism.

It is not the amount of clothes you have, where they come from, or how expensive they are that matters. There are a wide variety of discount stores, stores that sell slightly worn or used clothing, and a vast number of stores with professional-looking clothes at reasonable prices. What is important is that they are clean, tailored to fit you, and appropriate for the task. Clothes need not be expensive in order to look professional, and cost should never be an excuse for looking unprofessional. Think before you put on a tie or blouse that has a stain, a shirt that is ripped, or a hem that is pinned. Suits, shirts, sport coats, and pants should be clean, tailored, and pressed. If you forget one day, that will be the day you run into someone you wish you hadn't!

The way you dress ultimately impacts your brand, that is, the way people perceive you, as well as your company's brand. Perceptions are formed about your level of expertise.

On the Side

"I couldn't believe it. On casual day I wore my jeans and tennis shoes like everyone else. My boss came up to me and said, "Nice dirty Keds," referring to my tennis shoes. I didn't think anyone would notice that they were a little dirty. I am now 100 percent aware of the fact that what I wear and how I present myself has a tremendous impact on how others see me. I now really take care of my appearance, especially on 'casual day.'"

—A manager with Nestlé

Ask Yourself These Crucial Questions

» What is my current position? What position would I like to have?

» Do I feel more confident when I take the time to think about what I'm wearing?

» Whom will I be seeing today? If I run into a client, a prospective employer, or the president of my company, will I feel professional?

Tips

» It is important to dress for where you want to be in your career, not for where you are. The people who command the most respect are the people who look as though they respect themselves.

» Remember that your clothing projects your image and has a direct effect on how others perceive you.

» Make sure your clothes fit properly. If not, alter them yourself or have them altered. Clothes that are too tight look cheap, no matter how expensive they are.

» Suits should last at least three to five years.

» Always opt for quality over quantity.

» A coat of clear nail polish applied daily protects colored nail polish longer.

» Keep clear nail polish with you to stop a run from further damaging your hosiery.

» Save your plastic dry cleaning bags and use them when packing for a trip. This will help prevent your clothes from creasing.

» Take your clothes to the dry cleaner only when necessary.

» Check your clothes for dirt and stains before you put them back in your closet. That way, the only clothes in your closet will be clean clothes, and people won't focus on the spot that you forgot about when you hung up the item.

» Your clothing should fit your lifestyle. Do not buy clothes that are just going to sit in your closet. You should feel great in whatever you buy. If you don't love it, don't buy it.

» When you buy something, be sure that you'll be able to wear that item at least 10 times.

♦ If you are a smoker, you should have your clothes cleaned more often than nonsmokers to help get rid of the smell of stale smoke. After each wearing, wash as many items as you can. Note that fabric and hair absorb the smell of smoke, and the odor of perspiration and smoke can make things smell rotten or sour.

Professional Dress for Men

It is critical for men to pay attention to their attire and how it fits. Many of the gentlemen we have worked with do not think they need to focus on their attire in the workplace. They put it fairly far down on the priority list. A man may be highly intelligent, but if his suit sleeves are too long, he'll look sloppy. That impression carries over to work. We suggest to our male clients that if they are not sure what to do, they should go to a store that can help and guide.

Interesting Study

Do you think men who are well-dressed are seen as more successful, smarter, and more professional? A study by Kelton Research showed that is the case but that approximately 75 percet of men feel they are not dressed professionally the majority of time. The interviews revealed the following statistics:

> 91 percent of respondents felt that a man who dresses well appears to be more physically attractive than he is.

> 75 percent of respondents felt that men who dress well are actually more professionally successful.

> 22 percent of men felt that if they knew how to improve their dress, they would make more money.

All of this shows that appearance can impact your success due to a positive perception from others in the work environment.[1]

Research conducted by the British Physiological Society on first impressions is in line with the previous study. They also found that people perceive success in others who are well dressed. In one study, they asked people to rate a man who was well-dressed and one who was not. The well-dressed man was seen as confident and more successful. The raters did not realize it was the same man in both pictures.

Other research has shown that well-dressed individuals are seen as more successful, earning more money, and accomplishing more in their careers. This is true especially when compared to those who look sloppy. The research shows that it is not only what people perceive from the outside, but also how we feel on the inside. Northwestern University's studies support that and show that when people feel good in what they are wearing, it can affect their attitude, behavior, and overall demeanor.[2]

General Guidelines

- Your hair should look freshly combed or brushed all day. If your hair is hard to manage, there are many products on the market. Find what works well for you.

- All facial hair should be barbered or clean-shaven. Beards and mustaches should be groomed regularly. In some companies, facial hair is frowned upon and is not considered professional. Know the culture of your company.

- The hair on the back of your neck should be clean-shaven. When you are getting your hair cut, make sure you remind your barber or hairdresser to shave your neck.

- Your nose and ear hair should be trimmed regularly. You can purchase electric trimmers that make this job easier. Check yourself weekly.

- You may find it helpful to wear an undershirt. Undershirts help absorb perspiration and odor. You will find that they keep you cooler in the summer and warmer in the winter.

» Your shirts should be clean and pressed. Your collars should be treated, if necessary. Ask your dry cleaner to pay special attention to your collars because not all cleaners do this regularly. No matter how hot it is outside, wear long-sleeved shirts under your suits. You should have three to five shirts for each suit. White, pastels, and pinstripes are acceptable. Your brighter shirts should be kept for casual wear. Shirtsleeves should extend half an inch beyond the sleeve of your suit. They should never be longer than that.

» If you wear a vest, it should fit comfortably and not gap at the armholes.

» Your tie should fall between the middle and the bottom of your belt buckle. Be aware of what is trendy and what is professional regarding length. Know your environment and do what is appropriate.

» Silk ties are best. However, a blend that looks like silk is acceptable. Knot sizes for ties change with trends. Bow ties are acceptable as well.

» Keep your ties that have cartoons or slogans for nonbusiness wear.

» Your pants should break slightly over your shoes. The back of your pants should hit the top of the heels of your shoes. Your pants should be pressed after each wearing. One of the best investments you can make is a pants press. It can save you hundreds of dollars on dry cleaning. Pant cuffs go in and out of style. If you prefer them, cuffs should be kept about two inches deep, and you should still have a break in your slacks.

» Wool is the best fabric for suits. It lasts longer, doesn't wrinkle, and doesn't ball up easily.

» Suits, sport coats, and pants should be appropriate for your body proportions and fit comfortably. Have your suits altered professionally. The sleeves of your jackets should be sewn in rather than stapled or glued and should reach your wrist joint. They should not hike up when you lift your arms. If necessary, have the sleeves altered so they fit you properly. When you cup your hand at the bottom of your jackets, the bottom edge of the sleeves should fall in the crease of your cupped fingers.

▶ Double-breasted jackets go in and out of style. Look at the people in management in your company and see if other men are wearing them. Some companies do not consider them conservative enough for management personnel.

▶ Jackets with single vents are more traditional. However, in today's business environments, jackets that have one vent, two vents, or no vents at all are considered professional.

▶ The color of your socks should either match your shoes or slacks, or be appropriately stylish with a design that may be fun yet still professional. Fun socks may even be a way to differentiate your brand. Socks should be long enough so that when you are seated, no bare skin is showing. If you have a problem with your socks falling down, buy longer socks.

▶ Your shoes should be polished and match your belt. There are two-toned belts on the market (e.g., brown on one side and black on the other, or black and brown intertwined) that can make this easier for you. Check for scuffmarks weekly. Brown, black, and cordovan are considered the most professional colors to wear. Shoes that look worn can ruin the professional image you want others to have of you.

▶ Always wear a belt with pants that have belt loops. If your belt is marked from losing or gaining weight, take shoe polish and polish it. If that is not enough to make it look new, either take the belt to a shoemaker to have it refinished or buy a new belt. Old, worn-out belts tend to make people look sloppy.

» Cologne should be used sparingly. If you smell it on yourself, you are probably wearing too much.

» Your fingernails should be kept short, manicured, and clean.

» Wedding rings, school rings, or a small gold ring on your ring finger are acceptable.

Professional Dress for Women

In the business world today, women do not need to look like their male counterparts. Women have many different options for looking professional and feminine. There is one important question that you should ask yourself each time you get dressed for work: Do I want to be considered successful and professional, or do I want to look sexy? If you want to get ahead in the world of business, dress appropriately.

On the Side

"I received a call from a client asking us to coach a woman in his organization about her attire and how it was affecting her career. Keep in mind, their environment is edgy but professional and somewhat conservative. The woman was in her thirties and had done well there but could not figure out why she was not getting promoted. The problem was one that everyone else saw but would not tell her. She dressed as though she were going out on a date on a Saturday night. Her appearance was sexy, not professional. It was distracting to both men and women in the organization. She would go to a meeting with a lot to contribute, but people would walk out of the meeting discussing how they could see her bra through her shirt. The bottom line was that they were not going to think about promoting her until she started dressing the part of the role. The worst part of the situation was that it had been occurring for at least a year. No one internally would say anything to the young woman, but it was stalling her career."

—Image Dynamics executive coach

General Guidelines

» Your hair should look freshly brushed and combed. Long hair looks more professional when it is pulled back or in a relaxed style. Hair that is heavily teased does not project a professional image.

» A small amount of makeup is preferable and considered more professional than no makeup at all. Mascara, blush, and lipstick should be worn daily. Most women look as though they haven't taken the time to put themselves together without them.

» Make sure your shirts or blouses are clean and pressed at all times and not too tight. See-through shirts or blouses are never considered professional. If you perspire heavily, watch for marks under the armpits. Do not wear shirts that are stained.

» The length of your skirt needs to be appropriate for the style you are wearing, your age, and your weight. A short skirt should be one to two inches above or below the knee, and a long skirt should be two to three inches above the ankle. You should have your clothes altered to fit your body when necessary.

Interesting Study

We have worked with many women who do not like to wear makeup and swear that it makes no difference. Unfortunately for them, studies show differently. In a couple of studies people were asked rate how trustworthy, likeable, attractive, and intelligent women were. These women wore either very little, moderate, or heavy makeup. They found that women who had no makeup on were not rated as highly as women who were wearing a professional amount of makeup. In fact, the women wearing moderate amounts of makeup were rated much more positively, and seen as friendlier and more intelligent.[3]

- Women's slacks require no break. If you need to have your slacks altered, keep the hem the same length all the way around at the bottom.

- The sleeves of your jackets should be altered to fit your arm length and should end at your wrist joint.

- In most corporate settings, hosiery must be worn at all times. It is best to stay with shades of beige, black, and navy. The shade of your hose should match or blend with your skirt, pants, or shoes. An extra pair of hose and a bottle of clear nail polish in your purse or briefcase is a necessity in the event of a tear or run in your hosiery.

- Opaque tights are acceptable in cold weather. They should be worn with skirts or dresses. Thin, long socks are acceptable when worn with pants. They should look similar to panty hose. Black, navy, or brown with no designs are preferable and more practical.

- Try to match or blend your shoes with your clothing. Spectator shoes are acceptable, as well. Shoes that have been dyed to match an outfit are not professional. White shoes get dirty quickly and have a tendency to look old. Wearing shoes that are inappropriate can ruin your entire outfit. Check your shoes for scuff marks regularly and polish your shoes weekly. The heels of your shoes should never look worn. Heel height should not exceed two inches.

- If you are wearing a belt, it should match or blend with your shoes. Belts that are black, brown, navy, or cream are the most professional looking.

- Often, the right belt pulls an outfit together. Belt loops are not a prerequisite for women when it comes to accessorizing with a belt! If your belt is marked from losing or gaining weight, use shoe polish to polish it. If this doesn't work, take the belt to a shoemaker and have it refinished or buy a new one.

❧ Perfume should be worn in small amounts only. When you perspire, the scent is doubled. If you are able to smell the perfume after you have applied it, you have used too much.

❧ Your fingernails should be manicured and clean. Your nails should be kept relatively short. Nails that are too long do not look professional. Acrylic nails should not be too thick or too long. Nail polish that is too bright or has sparkles is inappropriate. Nail polish that is chipped or smudged makes a poor impression. Nail art is never considered professional.

❧ Earrings that are small or medium sized look professional. They should not have a lot of stones or be too glittery. Rings should be worn only on the ring finger or your pinkie. Religious symbols, ankle bracelets, ear cuffs, and visible pierced body parts (excluding pierced ears) are not appropriate. If your ears are pierced, do not wear more than one earring in each ear.

Business Attire

Business attire is the most conservative form of dress. It requires a full suit with jacket and either pants or a skirt. When you are meeting someone for the first time, whether for an interview or with a potential customer, business attire is considered the most professional form of dress. In a conservative professional environment, the only situation in which you might not wear business attire is if you wear a uniform or have discussed the issue of what to wear prior to your first meeting.

Caveat: this obviously varies in different lines of work and geographical locations around the world. Having an awareness of what is appropriate and what will differentiate you is critical to your success. Look for examples within your company or industry and model success.

Conservative Business Attire for Men

> ▷ Wear a starched dress shirt.

> ▷ Wear a suit rather than sport coat and slacks.

> ▷ Accessorize with a leather belt, matching shoes, and a conservative tie.

> ▷ Wear a watch with a leather or bracelet band. Sport watches are not appropriate for business attire.

> ▷ Shoes should be shined dress shoes not soft leather ones like duck shoes.

Conservative Business Attire for Women

> ▷ Wear a tailored suit that has a matching or coordinating skirt. Conservative dresses that do not show cleavage, are not glittery, and are not too tight are also considered appropriate. If a dress is suitable to wear to an evening holiday party, it still may not be appropriate for work.

> ▷ You can accessorize with a scarf or a belt that accents your suit or dress.

> ▷ Your shoes should be leather. Closed toe shoes are more professional in a conservative environment.

> ▷ Wear a watch with a leather or bracelet band. Sports watches are not appropriate for business attire.

Business Casual

Professionalism and consistency are two of the most important factors to consider when you are dressing for success. There is a big difference between casual dressing and sloppy dressing. Do not damage your professional image by looking sloppy. Your dress should be consistent with the image you are trying to project.

Business casual is similar to business attire except that a jacket is not required. Business casual is not what you would wear when lounging around your house, watching a ball game, or shopping at the grocery store. It is one level of dress below business attire but still requires that you be dressed for business.

Business Casual for Men

> If possible, do not wear the pants from your suits as they will get worn out before the jacket.

> Do not wear cotton slacks or jeans.

> Long-sleeved, well-pressed shirts, silk-type sweaters, or shirts with open collars and jackets are acceptable.

> Leather shoes and dress socks should be worn at all times.

Business Casual for Women

> Pantsuits are appropriate for business casual attire.

> Slacks with silk or cotton blouses or with twin sweater sets are acceptable.

> Scarves and other types of conservative accessories may be used.

> Shoes should be appropriate in your workspace. If business casual still means closed toe and heel, then stay within those parameters. If wearing open-toe shoes, make sure that your feet are pedicured. People look at shoes immediately, so make sure your shoes represent your brand, even in a casual or business casual environment.

Casual Attire

Each company and culture has a different interpretation of casual attire. As you have read, your expertise, confidence, and professionalism are communicated through your attire. Do not let your level of casual attire affect your career just to be comfortable. Find out if your company has a policy regarding casual dress. If there are written rules, make sure you read them carefully.

Casual Attire for Both Men and Women

> ▷ Find out whether denim is acceptable.

> ▷ Cotton or corduroy pants or skirts are acceptable.

> ▷ Blouses and shirts may be made of cotton or knit fabrics.

> ▷ Casual shoes may be worn.

— Interesting Study —

Do you realize that the way you dress could affect your bottom line? How about your company's results? The *Journal of American Academy of Business* found that you actually can affect how others perceive you and your company.[4] Think about how you dress because it could affect your outcomes.

Many companies will allow you to wear some of the following items, but your choices should be well thought out to match your brand and your goals.

> ▷ Jeans should not fit too tightly. They should never be faded, have holes, or have frayed edges.

> ▷ Shorts should come almost to the knee. Walking shorts or Bermuda shorts are best. Short shorts should never be worn.

> ▷ Tight-fitting pants such as leggings are never appropriate when they are so tight you can see undergarments or cellulite.

> ▷ T-shirts (without logos) must be clean and pressed. Muscle shirts should never be worn.

> Tennis shoes, other types of sport shoes, or sandals may be worn if acceptable in your company.

> If the toes of your shoes are open, your toenails should be pedicured.

Tips

▶ It is always better to be overdressed than underdressed.

▶ If it is acceptable to wear jeans, make sure they are in good condition.

▶ Your socks must be clean and free of holes.

▶ If you are wearing a T-shirt, make sure it is not wrinkled or faded. T-shirts have a way of getting the "worn" look quickly. If your collar is askew, iron it before wearing the shirt.

▶ When you wear tennis shoes or other types of sneakers, make sure they are polished and clean. White shoe polish or a shoeshine shop can refurbish them and make your shoes look like new.

After-Hours Business Attire for Both Men and Women

▶ Remember, business after hours is still business.

▶ Women should never wear anything that is too short, too low-cut, or too tight.

▶ Daytime suits can always be dressed up with a different blouse and different accessories in order to become more appropriate for the evening.

▶ Men always look best in darker suits when they are conducting after-hours business.

Big Blunder 10 \ Lacking Meeting Etiquette

Decide what you want, decide what you are willing to exchange for it. Establish your priorities and go to work.

—H. L. Hunt

Leading, participating in, or attending a meeting should always be viewed as an opportunity to exhibit your professionalism. Whether you are a participant or the facilitator really doesn't matter. When people leave the meeting, they will leave it with an impression of you. Their impression, whether positive or negative, will affect whether you work together and, if you do work together, how well you work with one another. It is very important that the message attendees get is the message you want to send. Whether you lead a meeting or are a participant, you must know ahead of time the impressions that

On the Side

"A client of ours called the office and sounded desperate. 'What should I do? I just got out of a client meeting and one of our team members took out his nail clippers and started clipping his fingernails.'"

—Sales manager, Fortune 100 company

you want others at the meeting to take away with them. You need to think about this carefully before the meeting ever starts.

Ask Yourself These Crucial Questions

▶ Am I fully prepared for the meeting?

▶ Does each person have an agenda for the meeting, or am I planning to hand out the agenda once we are there?

▶ Do I know where to stand or sit in order to have the greatest impact on the others in the room?

Leading a Meeting

▶ You must be clear, concise, and articulate.

▶ The goal of the meeting should be identified at the beginning.

▶ Each participant should have an agenda; you may need to send it out ahead of time.

▶ The meeting should begin and end on time.

▶ Do not fidget with your materials, your fingernails, your hair, and so forth.

▶ Do not put unnecessary materials on the table (for example, purse, briefcase, coat, and so on). In most instances, a pad, a pen, an agenda, and any backup materials are sufficient.

▶ Show an appreciation for others' points of view.

▶ Have more than the exact number of handouts and preview materials you think you will need. The five-plus rule is a good one to remember: think about the maximum number of participants you expect to attend and add five more.

▶ Make eye contact with each of the participants. Scanning the room isn't sufficient.

▶ Make sure your body language is inviting. People will not feel comfortable asking you questions if they feel intimidated.

▶ Be careful that you don't give anyone the message that what he or she has said is unimportant. People need to feel that you have heard them, that you appreciate what they have said, and that their contribution is valued. Never argue with a coworker or a customer. If there are areas of disagreement, suggest a meeting after the larger meeting is over to discuss the issue in more depth.

Seating Arrangements

▶ Make sure that you can see everyone at the meeting without having to turn your head more than 180 degrees. If you find that you have to do so, ask some of the participants to move to other seats. Your team can be interspersed, but the presenters must be able to address everyone at the same time.

▶ Let the customer know if you will be or might be bringing others to the meeting.

▶ When the point person sets up an appointment and another team member attends the meeting, it is important that the point person deliver the majority of the presentation. Any changes in this format (that is, if someone other than the point person will be presenting) require some communication prior to the meeting.

▶ Introduce your coworkers to your clients.

▶ If you are in a conference room, remember that the seats on either side of the person leading the meeting are considered the most significant.

▶ Do not sit in cliques, do not break away into small groups, and do not spread out during a meeting unless you need to do so in order to function.

Participating in a Meeting

▶ Always arrive on time.

- Feel free to participate, but do not participate merely to draw attention to yourself.
- Don't be afraid to ask questions that you feel are relevant to the point being made.
- Before you begin to speak, wait at least three seconds after the previous speaker has finished.
- Do not talk to your neighbor while another person is speaking.
- Confine all discussion to the situation at hand. Do not discuss problems on the side.
- Keep a pleasant or interested look on your face.
- Pay attention.
- Speak up.
- Remember to be clear and concise.

Tips

- Look interested and stay alert.
- Turn off all computers and cell phones.
- State the ground rules and your expectations for the meeting.
- Give credit where credit is due. Use "we" instead of "I" when appropriate.
- Thinking and planning ahead of time is most important. Gather all the files and materials you feel are applicable and lay them out ahead of time. That way, you reduce the chance of forgetting something on the day of the meeting.
- If you are dealing with numbers or sales, have a calculator on hand.
- Take time to process notes after the meeting.
- Always come to meetings well-prepared. If you don't, you can be sure that others will notice!

Big Blunder 11 \ Being Unprepared for Interviews

Luck is when opportunity meets preparedness.

—Unknown

When you come to an interview unprepared, be aware of what it may cost you. Sometimes the price you will pay is not getting the job! Preparation for an interview should start the moment you decide on the company for which you want to work and the type of work you want to do for them. You need to plan well ahead of time. Think about what you know about the company, what they think they need, what you think they need, and why you feel they need you.

At a glance, Sue didn't think she would fit into the organization.

Your confidence in yourself and your competence to do the job are revealed during an interview. First impressions are crucial for job success. Interviewers decide on your competency to do the job on the basis of their initial impression of you. Remember, 55 percent of the impression you make is through nonverbal communication. Your attitude, your body language, what you wear, what you bring with you, and how well you present yourself and your information are important. Have complete control over the impression the interviewer gets from you. Your attitude, your attire, and your confidence in yourself are things that are in your control. Don't give the interviewer any opportunities to focus negatively on something over which you have control. Prospective employers are looking for confident and competent people who can do the job well. Being well-prepared for an interview can keep you giant steps ahead of the competition.

On the Side

"We put an advertisement in the paper for an open position and we received hundreds of résumés. We filled the position almost immediately. However, a subsequent résumé seemed outstanding. We called the applicant and arranged an interview. We thought, 'We need to find a job for her! She's just perfect for our company.' She came for the interview wearing a short black skirt, a T-shirt, and sandals without panty hose. If she had known more about our company, we would have spent more time talking to her and we might have given her a job. During the interview she mentioned that she had been on many interviews, but no one had called her back."

—Kim Zoller, president; and Kerry Preston, partner,
Image Dynamics

This applicant had an excellent résumé and was very capable and competent. However, she shot herself in the foot each time she went on an interview because she was unprepared and inappropriately dressed. It is important to research the company ahead of time. Being unprepared for an interview can be expensive!

Ask Yourself These Crucial Questions

» What do I want the outcome of the interview to be?

» How do I want the interviewer(s) to perceive me?

» What can I do to prepare myself for the interview?

» What will make me feel more confident when I go in for the interview?

Dressing for Your Interview

Wear business attire unless specifically asked to wear business casual. Even if you are asked to wear business casual, make sure you are well-dressed and on the dressier side of business casual.

Women

> Suits: Wear a skirt suit or a completely matched pantsuit. You can never go wrong choosing the skirt suit option.

> Blouses: Wear a blouse that is freshly pressed and that cannot be seen through.

> Hosiery: Wearing hosiery is a *must*. Mesh stockings or other types of decorative hosiery are not appropriate for interviewing. Choose a shade of hose that is beige, black, or navy.

> Shoes: Wear shoes that are freshly polished and have no scuffmarks. A closed-toe, closed-heel shoe is most appropriate for the corporate environment. Heel height should be no greater than two inches. Black, brown, or navy shoes are best.

> Handbags: Use a leather handbag, if possible. Make sure your handbag is free of scratches or scuffs. Black, navy, or brown is best.

> Belts: Wear a belt that matches your shoes or the fabric of your suit. Decorative belts (that is, fancy buckles, jeweled, and so on) are not appropriate for interviewing.

> Scarves should be color coordinated and enhance the suit.

> Jewelry should not be too loud or showy. Pins should not have a lot of colored stones or be overly large (no bigger than an inch and a half). No more than two rings (with an engagement ring and wedding band counting as one) should be worn. Rings should be worn on only your ring or pinkie fingers.

> Earrings should not be too big or dangly. Wear only one earring per ear! Wearing multiple earrings is not professional.

> Bracelets should not jingle. Ankle bracelets should not be worn.

> Watches should have bracelet or leather bands. Sport watches are not appropriate.

Men

> Suits: Wear a suit rather than a sport coat and pants. Suits should be somewhat conservative. Navy or gray are best.

> Shirts: Wear a shirt that is freshly pressed. White or light blue shirts are most appropriate. Do not wear shirts that have patterns (that is, heavily striped, plaid, paisley, and so on) or are colored (that is, bright blue, yellow, pink, red, and so on).

> ⸢ Ties: Wear a conservative tie (i.e., not too bright in color or with too much of a pattern).

> ⸢ Shoes: Wear shoes that are freshly polished and have no scuffmarks.

> ⸢ Belts: If your trousers have belt loops, be sure to wear a belt! Your belt should match your shoes.

What to Bring

▶ Both men and women should carry a briefcase or a portfolio. Leather is preferable.

▶ If carrying a briefcase, do not carry a handbag.

▶ Keys should be put in your briefcase, handbag, or portfolio. Do not put them in your pocket.

▶ Your resume should be ready for perusal. There should be no stains or creases on it.

▶ Have a pen and a pad of paper with you at all times.

Body Language

▶ When an interviewer comes to greet you, smile, make eye contact, and use a firm and professional handshake. (For more specific information, see Chapter 2.)

▶ Stand straight and tall. Do not slouch or cross your arms. You want to send a message that you are open, prepared, and ready to get down to business.

▶ Be energetic and excited about the opportunity.

▶ Do not wring your hands. It sends a message of nervousness and discomfort.

▶ Try to mirror the interviewer's position (for example, if he or she is sitting back, you should be sitting back; if he or she is sitting forward, then you should be sitting forward as well).

➤ Do not tap your feet or shake your leg. Keep your legs together.

➤ Do not cross your arms. Keep them in an open position.

➤ Do not fidget with your pen, pencil, hair, pins, and so forth.

What to Say

➤ Speak in positive terms. Do not bring up negative situations that you might have experienced in the past.

➤ Be prepared with at least three questions to ask the interviewer(s). *Never* ask about money during the first interview.

➤ Be comfortable talking about the research you have done and how it relates to what you will do and how the company will benefit.

How and Where to Sit

➤ Do not sit until you are invited to do so.

➤ Do not touch anything on the interviewer's desk. Ask permission to move something if necessary.

➤ Keep your posture erect. Do not slouch!

Follow Up

➤ At the end of the interview, ask the interviewer when you can follow up regarding their decision.

➤ Send a handwritten thank-you note the day of the interview. Personalize it by mentioning something you discussed during the interview.

➤ When three or fewer people interview you, write each interviewer a personal note. When more than three people interview you, send the person who was your point of contact a note and ask him or her to thank the other interviewers for you. Be sure to mention the names of the other interviewers.

Example of a Follow-Up Note

Dear Mr. Jones,

    It was a pleasure meeting you. Thank you for taking the time to discuss the [name of position]. It sounds extremely interesting. I am looking forward to the opportunity to work with you and [company name]. Thank you for considering me.

Sincerely yours,

Kim Zoller

Big Blunder 12 > Using Poor Telephone Etiquette and Protocol

When people talk, listen completely. Most people never listen.

—Ernest Hemingway

Many companies conduct the majority of their business over the telephone. Even though you may not be able to see the person to whom you are talking, and they cannot see you, each of you can still hear how involved the other person is in the conversation. Many people think that because they are good at multitasking, they can work on other tasks while on the phone. Other people know when you are doing something else! You need to listen carefully to how

On the Side

"I was talking to a coworker who I could tell was not listening to a word I had to say. It was frustrating me and so I decided to have some fun with it. I started saying off the wall things to him and all I heard back was, 'Uh huh. That's interesting.' I realized his attention (or lack of it) discredited his overall professionalism."

—E-marketing manager, Fortune 500 company

the person on the other end of the line is reacting to you. Telephone conversations are opportunities to build your relationships. You cannot do that unless you are involved in the conversation and focused on what the person on the other end is saying.

Ask Yourself These Crucial Questions

▶ Do I get frustrated and insulted when someone asks me to repeat myself numerous times?

▶ Can I tell when someone is smiling on the other end of the telephone?

▶ Is it easier and more pleasant to talk to someone whose attention is on me 100 percent of the time?

Answering the Telephone

▶ Whenever possible, answer by the third ring.

▶ Speak clearly and slowly at all times.

▶ Before starting the conversation, state your name and your company name.

▶ Smile when you answer the phone. It helps keep your voice friendly and welcoming. Keeping a mirror at your desk and looking at it while you are on the phone can be helpful.

▶ Have a pen and paper in front of you. Always be prepared to take notes.

Making Telephone Calls

▶ Make your calls early in the day. People are more likely to be available and ready to talk in the mornings. If they are not available, you are more likely to receive a return call on the same day.

▶ Before you pick up the telephone, know what you want to say and smile as you say it.

▶ Before beginning a conversation, state your full name and the name of your company.

▶ Always ask, "Do you have a moment?"

▶ It is extremely important to get to the point of your call quickly. Be concise. Time is money.

▶ Thank the person for his or her time.

▶ Always confirm when you are going to speak with each other for follow-up. This helps to set the stage for future telephone calls.

Leaving Messages

▶ You should know what you want to say and how you are going to say it before you pick up the telephone.

▶ Be clear, concise, and articulate.

▶ State your full name and the name of your company. Be sure the message you leave is sufficiently detailed so there is no confusion about what you need the other person to do.

▶ Speak slowly. Many people speak too quickly, which makes messages difficult to understand. It is helpful to write your phone number down as you are leaving your message. This ensures that the person receiving the message has time to write it down correctly. People respond to calls 90 percent faster if they have your phone number in front of them and do not have to look it up!

Returning Calls

▶ Return calls within 24 hours.

▶ If you cannot return telephone calls within that time period, let callers know by leaving a detailed message on your voicemail.

Staying Focused

» When you are on the telephone, do not doodle. Doodling takes your attention away from the person to whom you are talking.

» Do not use your computer while you are on the telephone, unless necessary.

» When you are on the phone, keep the number of interruptions to an absolute minimum. Interruptions, no matter how infrequent, send a message of disinterest and disrespect.

» Keep your voice positive, listen carefully, and respond appropriately. Being there and knowing that you are truly listening to them makes people want to do business with you.

Big Blunder 13 \ Choosing the Wrong Gift

The man who will use his skill and constructive imagination to see how much he can give for a dollar, instead of how little he can give for a dollar, is bound to succeed.

—Henry Ford

Gift giving in business often becomes part of our jobs. Holidays, weddings, births, birthdays, and other occasions are usually celebrated in the workplace. Finding the right gift for a boss, colleague, or client can be challenging. Whoever said it is better to give than to receive, underestimated the difficulty and importance of selecting the perfect gift.

Gifts must be chosen with care and thoughtfulness. The gifts we give as well as how we present them are a direct reflection of us. With that in mind, use the age-old custom of gift giving as an opportunity to make a favorable and lasting impression on the recipient. If your company is paying for the gift, find out whether it has a gift-giving policy that limits expense or offers guidelines. If you are giving a gift to a client, make sure you check your client's policy on receiving gifts.

If you are fortunate enough to be on the receiving end the next holiday season, we offer one final tip: Send thank-you notes to everyone who gives you a gift. Nothing beats a simple handwritten thank-you note sent three to five days after you receive your gift.

On the Side

"I had just started a new job and a senior colleague gave me a holiday gift. I reciprocated by giving the person a very elaborate bottle of wine. I was so embarrassed when the thank-you letter came back stating how kind, and that perhaps they would put a drop into some special dish they might cook. I can assure you that I always find out what is appropriate before I give a gift!"

—CPA and tax accountant

Ask Yourself These Crucial Questions

▶ What are some of the recipient's interests or hobbies?

▶ How does this gift reflect on my image?

▶ Will the recipient be comfortable receiving this gift?

Gift Selection

Simple gifts such as candles, paperweights, picture frames, pen or pencil sets, or music are usually best. A gift should be somewhat personal because you want the recipient to know that you gave the gift some thought. However, the gift should not be too personal and should not embarrass the recipient in any way. If you know the interests or hobbies of the recipient, choose a gift with that theme. Gag gifts are not usually a good idea because they might offend the recipient. Another option is to purchase a gift on behalf of a group of your colleagues. In this way, you can brainstorm gift ideas and perhaps increase the value of the gift itself. A charitable donation made in a client's name is a wonderful gesture and a great idea for those clients who have a "no gift" policy. The amount of the donation should not be disclosed. The honor is that a donation has been made in your client's name. Choose a charity that you feel will not be offensive to anyone or one in which the client has previously expressed an interest.

Coffee mugs, T-shirts, pens, or other items that can be personalized with your company logo are popular as well. When trying to set yourself apart from the competition, pick unusual items that would appeal to individual tastes. For example, a soft briefcase, some golf balls, a garment bag, or a gym bag might work really well. Many wineries are willing to private label their wines with a company logo on the label, if appropriate. Gift certificates to new restaurants are a great idea. However, keep in mind that once the certificate is used, it's the kind of gift that is easily forgotten.

Give a gift that fits the individual. For example, giving wine to a nondrinker won't go over well, and a gym bag for someone who doesn't work out doesn't serve any purpose.

Gifts for Employees

Assistants must be given a gift. The number of years of service should be taken into account when thinking about the gift. If you are giving gifts to other employees in the office, no one should be left out. All the employees should be given an equal or comparable gift.

Suggestions:

▷ Candy, perfume (make sure you know what scent the person prefers), or scarves	▷ Jewelry (for an assistant who has been with you for a substantial amount of time)
▷ Aftershave (make sure you know what scent the person prefers) or ties for men	▷ Appointment books and calendars
▷ Gift certificates	▷ Gift baskets of food or bath products

Gifts for Employers

Employees can give gifts to their employers. The gift does not have to be expensive and should not be too personal. Joint gifts from an entire staff are a great idea. They are less embarrassing for the employer and will cost each employee less than an individual gift.

Suggestions:

> a bottle of wine (if appropriate)

> a gift certificate for two to a restaurant

> a scarf or a tie

> personalized stationery

Gifts for Coworkers

When exchanging gifts with coworkers, it is important that no one is left out and that no one feels alienated. If you plan on giving gifts to a few people only, do so at lunch, and not on company time. Some companies have employees draw a name out of a hat and set a limit for spending. This is a great idea; everyone can be included, and the cost is the same across the board.

Suggestions:

> Bath products	> Candles
> Wine	> Cigars
> Ties	> Stationery
> Cooking accessories	> Movie tickets
> Picture frames	> CDs or books

Frequently Asked Questions

Q. Can a gift be too extravagant? What is the appropriate amount to spend?

A. The amount you spend will depend on your personal budget, your previous experiences, and your common sense. If your company is paying for the gift, find out whether there is a gift-giving policy that limits expense or offers guidelines. No matter who is paying, we recommend spending approximately $30 on a classic, thoughtful gift. Food gifts such as fruit baskets, popcorn tins, specialty candies, or business accessories such as pens, calendars, and books are all good ideas. For an extra special touch, have your company logo embossed or printed on the item. Remember that all packages must be neatly wrapped. The gift you give is a reflection of you.

Q. Are there rules of etiquette when it comes to giving alcohol?

A. You should know your company policy regarding alcohol and the company policy of the recipient as well. Some companies prohibit the giving of alcohol under any circumstances. Consider the individual tastes of the person to whom you are giving the gift as well.

If you know the recipient is a wine connoisseur, then a bottle of wine is a thoughtful gift. Alternatives to giving wine or alcohol might include wine books, stemware, or novelty wine stoppers.

Big Blunder 14 \ Lacking Professionalism While Traveling

There are always opportunities through which businessmen can profit handsomely if they will only recognize and seize them.

—John Paul Getty

When you are traveling for business, it is important to keep in mind that you are representing yourself and your company. Business travel is the norm, and the opportunities to do business while traveling are endless. You never know whom you might meet. You need to be prepared for meeting all types of people and for networking with anyone who could affect your business, either positively or negatively.

Ask Yourself These Crucial Questions
» What is going to make me look and feel professional?

» If I run into someone with whom I work or my biggest client, how do I want them to perceive me?

» If I meet someone who is of value to my business or to myself personally, what kind of impression do I want him or her to take away from the encounter?

What to Take With You

» Briefcase

» Business cards

» Writing instruments

» Legal pad(s) for notes

» Books, magazines, and other reading material for business as well as pleasure

» Computer and accessories

» Toothbrush and breath mints

Protocol on the Plane

» Help when you see another passenger struggling with baggage.

» Be courteous, patient, and respectful of all airport personnel; it is not as easy to travel as it used to be.

» Understand that the people who are not on the aisle have needs too. They are not getting up to spite or inconvenience you.

On the Side

"I was on my way out of town for a business trip when I remembered that I needed to pick something up from my mentor's house. After opening the door, he looked at me and asked, 'Are you traveling like that?' I said, 'Yes. The seminar isn't until tomorrow so I thought I would travel comfortably.' I was wearing jeans and a cotton blouse. In a serious tone, he said, 'When you are traveling for business, the business starts before you leave your house. What you wear on the airplane, how you look, what you carry, and how you behave all represent who you are and what you do. If someone asks what company you work for, where you are going, and what you are going to do when you get there, making an apology for how you look is embarrassing and, even worse, it is really poor business technique.' I will never forget his advice. I have made some of my best contacts on business trips."

—Sales trainer

▶ Greet the people who are sitting next to you. You never know when an opportunity may present itself.

▶ Talk softly. Remember that others around you should not be disturbed.

▶ Know your limits regarding alcoholic beverages. Alcohol has an enhanced effect at higher altitudes.

▶ Assess your neighbors' willingness to have a conversation. Don't assume they want to talk or listen to your life story.

Tips

▶ Check your ticket carefully before the day of travel. Make sure everything is correct.

▶ Confirm everything (flights, hotel reservations, meetings, appointments, and so on) before you leave, even if you have confirmed them previously.

▶ Store your ticket in a safe place and remember where you put it.

▶ A good garment bag saves time.

▶ Put a small umbrella in your bag.

▶ Take an all-weather coat with a zip-in lining, just in case.

▶ Travel-size toiletries reduce bulk.

▶ A travel alarm keeps you in full control.

▶ Take extra hangers with you.

▶ Fold shirts and blouses around tissue or plastic bags to reduce wrinkling.

▶ Line the top and bottom of your bag(s) with plastic dry-cleaning bags.

▶ Tuck your socks and coiled belts inside your shoes for compact packing.

Big Blunder 15 〉Lacking Global Awareness and Maturity

The root of "going global" isn't an option reserved for executives at worldwide companies; it is an essential activity that every decision maker must perform to keep pace in today's world. Respectful and culturally appropriate behavior shows global awareness and business maturity. No two cultures are alike, and it is important to be flexible when in other environments. Global awareness empowers you to proactively adapt, innovate, and focus on strategic measures that drive achievement.

—David Goldsmith, president of the Goldsmith Organization

Our business community becomes increasingly smaller as we live and work in different countries that are part of a multi-national business environment. People want to work with others who have global awareness and understand a wide variety of views and practices.

In order to help its students and faculty appreciate differences, the University of Sheffield in London defines the following elements in their description of global awareness:

> ▷ Appreciating and respecting personal and cultural differences.

> ▷ Being aware of the diverse needs, feelings, and views of other people.

> ▷ Communicating and working with people from different countries and backgrounds.

> ▷ Understanding how world issues may affect society and people's lives.

> ▷ Being active in society at local, national, and international levels.[1]

Ask Yourself These Crucial Questions

▶ Do I know if you I am ego-centric and ethnocentric and feel that what I do is what everyone does or should do?

▶ Do I know how to manage cross-cultural situations?

On the Side

"Last year, when I was in India, I realized why there is a communication gap when it comes to agreement. My North American clients were frustrated because their Indian counterparts agreed to do the discussed work, yet ultimately did not deliver. My Indian clients were frustrated because their North American counterparts did not understand that they had not agreed to do the work but had agreed to hear what needed to be done and look into it to see if they could deliver the work. Their expectations on how they each responded to making an agreement were completely different. Once they realized the nuances of each other's responses, they were able to communicate more effectively and, hence, lower that frustration."

—Kim Zoller, Image Dynamics

⏵ Have I thought about growing my relationships by growing my knowledge of my worldwide colleagues' cultural nuances?

Tips

⏵ Gather culture-specific information about the countries you work with most often. No one can know everything about every country, so do your homework for situations you will encounter just one time or on a regular basis.

⏵ Read about global happenings and news events.

⏵ Look for similarities and differences to enhance conversations.

⏵ Understand and learn the nuances of the language.

⏵ Slow down when communicating to ensure understanding.

⏵ Write down key points and clarify to make sure you are on the same page and mean the same thing.

⏵ Watch your humor and slang. These may be received in a completely different way than they were intended.

⏵ Learn the differences in addressing the person as it relates to him or her name.

⏵ Body language is different around the world; do not make any assumptions that what you do is normal and customary in other places.

⏵ Learn and adapt to business card protocol.

⏵ Learn the dining norms of the host country or the person you are hosting. The likelihood of them being different from yours is great.

⏵ Nurture the relationship in the comfort zone of the other person in his or her culture.

On the Side

"One of our clients, Joe, conducted a new-hire orientation. Joe recalled feeling completely embarrassed by one of his actions with his Japanese colleagues. Two senior executives from their headquarters in Japan were participating in the orientation meeting. Joe was facilitating a debrief conversation with the entire group and asked his Japanese colleague for input on the technology presentation. The room went silent and Joe's colleague did not offer his input. Joe felt extremely uncomfortable and moved on quickly as the room continued to be deathly silent. Later he learned that in Japan, the debrief and input occurs after the meeting is closed."

—Image Dynamics client

Big Blunder 16 \ The Unprofessional Intern

If you can dream it, you can do it.

—Walt Disney

Internships can be a wonderful opportunity to gain experience, learn about specific companies and job functions, and give you an edge over other job applicants. Take time to research fields and companies that interest you. Once you have landed your internship, remember to avoid actions that would prevent the employer from offering you a job in the future or giving you a positive recommendation.

In this chapter, our goal is to share practical advice and real sticky situations from former interns with suggestions on how to navigate them.

Internship Don'ts

➠ Arriving late to work in the morning.

➠ Wearing clothes that are not appropriate (too tight, wrinkled, or casual).

➠ Doing the least amount of work as possible.

▶ Spending time on personal phone calls, email, and social media sites.

▶ Failing to create ideas and deliver more than expected.

▶ Not taking initiative to help others.

▶ Neglecting to learn about other roles and departments within the company.

▶ Failing to build relationships and a network of contacts.

▶ Assuming your work was noticed as opposed to scheduling time to spotlight your work.

Real Sticky Situation 1
Dealing With an Emotionally Charged and Stubborn Intern

One of the projects my supervisor assigned was to work in a group of three with the two other interns in the office to create computer templates. This group project entailed the three of us to work separately at first to come up with a list of financial metrics we thought would be important to include in monitoring the company's financial soundness, and then meet as a group to merge our three versions of the template into a cohesive whole. During the group-meeting portion of the project, one of the interns in the group was very difficult to work with because he became very defensive and argumentative about his template and refused to listen to what the other members suggested. It reached the point where he was raising his voice and causing the other members of team to feel uncomfortable and frustrated as well.

Solution

I took a step back from the tense situation and reassessed why this fellow intern was feeling and acting this way. The group decided to take a short break from the meeting to calm down. When we reconvened, I changed my communication style to focus on the big-picture task at hand and allowed room for everyone in the group to have an equal chance to voice their opinion about each section of the template. I positively affirmed my group mates' ideas to make sure they knew that I valued their ideas, and tried to help broker compromise among the three of us to ensure that parts of each person's individual work was somehow included into the final template that we presented to our supervisor.

Real Sticky Situation 2
Staying Connected after a Completed Internship

When leaving an internship, many times the goal is to get an offer from the company. Managing communications to be remembered is in itself a sticky situation. I think it would be very useful for interns to have some guidance on how to maintain the network they are building through their internships after leaving.

Solution

Before leaving, I wrote all of my direct supervisors handwritten thank-you cards that I delivered to them in person or left on their desks. During the last few days of my internship, I also scheduled brief one-on-one meetings with my supervisors to ask them for feedback and constructive criticism of my work for them. I also sent the other interns and the communications department I was a part of separate emails thanking them and explaining how much I had valued working with them. Then, I connected with the people I had worked with on LinkedIn and asked the supervisor I had worked with most to write a recommendation. As I was working primarily in a digital media department, I felt it was appropriate to also connect with them and interact with them through Twitter; I would post new digital analytic tools I had found directed at their account or re-post industry news. I also followed their pages closely on Facebook, liking and engaging as I saw fit. I attended a product launch hosted by the company in New York City and live tweeted for them throughout. Finally, I applied for a full-time position and succeeded.

Real Sticky Situation 3
Bored, With Nothing to Do

Your employer just launched a new marketing campaign in May. You start your internship in mid-June, and your first two weeks are very busy with various assignments related to this campaign. You really enjoy the experience of being thrown into projects right away. However, halfway through your internship, things slow down, and your supervisor doesn't have a lot for you to do. She is also very busy with work that you cannot assist with and has not had a lot of time to think of new projects you can work on, so you are starting to get bored at work. On some days, you just surf the Internet and wait for the day to end. You are worried that the rest of your internship will be like this.

Solution

It is important for you to know what to do in this situation. Remember, there is always more than one right answer, so take time to think about your options before leaping into action. Go to your boss or manager and be clear and direct that you would like more to do. Without complaining or whining, remind them that you are there to learn as much as you can and are open to doing anything they need. Take your time before the discussion to look around and see what possible opportunities there are within your workspace so that you can suggest specific projects, such as conducting Internet research on specific topic recommendations.

Real Sticky Situation 4
Bait and Switch

Your internship is at a large nonprofit organization. In the interview and selection process, you met and largely interacted with the energetic and enthusiastic executive director. She seems as excited as you are about your working at the nonprofit. For the internship, however, the executive director explains that she will be very busy and therefore will assign one of her assistant directors to be your immediate supervisor. You are initially excited about the opportunity, but almost right away tension develops between you and your supervisor. She seems annoyed that she has to supervise and work with you. You have tried repeatedly to find polite but indirect ways to address the issue, but she seems totally resistant to your efforts. In addition, your work is not challenging or what you thought you were going to be doing.

Solution

There are multiple ways to procced. Regarding the executive director: get on her schedule to meet. Before you do that, be aware of her schedule and the timing of when she works. For instance, if she gets in early, schedule the appointment for early in the day, if you see that that's the best time to get her attention. Sit down with the director and, with no animosity or resentment in your voice, say something like this: "I'm very grateful for the position and I know you set the expectation that you were going to be extremely busy while I was here. I would really appreciate if you could take an hour a week to mentor me during my internship. I know that I have a lot to learn from you and I do not want to miss out on the opportunity." If the opportunity is given to you to meet with her, make sure you are well-prepared at every meeting with specific questions that will help your overall growth, not the specifics of the job you are doing during the internship.

The best way to handle this situation with your supervisor is to work hard at eliminating any tension between the two of you. It is important that you are respectful and accept the work, even though it is not challenging. If possible, push the work to a new level to create a challenge for yourself. It is important to get agreement from you supervisor about how you can meet her expectations. Ask how she will measure your efforts as a success. See solution to Real Sticky Situation 3 for more insight.

Real Sticky Situation 5
Bad Assumptions

You are working for a consulting company, and you have been asked to organize and analyze a large set of financial data on a client company. Your supervisor will be using the data in an important team meeting in a couple of days. It is your first project, and you want to show your employer that you are very capable and up to the challenge, but when you receive the data, you are unsure about exactly what you are supposed to do. You see that your supervisor is really busy and do not want to bother him, so you decide to just try to figure it out as best you can. When you present it to him, he tells you that the data was not organized or analyzed in the way he needed.

Solution

When in doubt, it is important to ask you supervisor for a few minutes of his or her time. Assumptions can only get you in trouble, especially when you have a short amount of time to make the best impression. The best solution is to go to your boss and ask for clarification. If you are not sure what to say or you are worried that he will feel that you were not paying attention when he assigned the project, say something like this: "I want to make sure that I do this exactly the way you would like it done. There are a few places where I may be making assumptions, and I want to make sure that I meet your expectations. Could we go through these areas in the data?" If after that conversation you present the data and the feedback is not to his liking, then ask him politely to give you specific feedback and details. Thank him for his feedback and redo the work. You will actually be training him how to present data to get the results he wants in the future.

Real Sticky Situation 6
Unclear Expectations

Before your internship began, you were told that you should be at work every morning at around 8 a.m. For the first few weeks, you arrive at work every morning by 8 a.m., but you notice that your coworkers do not usually arrive until 9 a.m. at the earliest. Furthermore, your supervisor does not generally get in until around 9 a.m. You generally have nothing to do for the first hour you're there because the supervisor tends to give you specific daily work.

Solution

It is important for you to go to your supervisor and clarify the hours and expectations. Ask what work should be done first thing in the morning. Let them know that you are open to coming in at 8 a.m., but you're just not sure of the expectation until he or she gets there and gives you your daily assignment. Keep in mind that people get extremely busy, and it may be a complete oversight. Just be careful in that situation to be open and receptive, not annoyed or frustrated. We cannot read minds, so asking clarifying questions aids in the communication process.

Chapter 17

Ask Kim and Kerry: Answers to Sticky Situations

In this Q&A section, we have compiled questions that come up on a regular basis with our clients. We approach every question with the "You did what?!" mentality: If at any time someone can turn around and say "You did what?!" in a situation, it has not been handled well. Think about what would be the most professional outcome, one that continues to build bridges and never burns them.

Q: What do I do when I am working on a project with a person who doesn't respond to my emails?

A: First, do not be the person who does not respond. Not responding to emails is unprofessional and remembered. It creates tension in relationships and feelings that can lead to a decline in business productivity or effectiveness with the other person. Keep in mind that there may be a time when you need something from that person in a hurry, and he will remember how you did or did not respond to him in a timely manner, if at all.

Back to the question: If you find that others are not responding to you, it is important to clarify timing and when you would like a response. If you have done that, think of another approach. Are your emails too long? Do they have the action in the subject line? Can you contact the person's assistant to help you? How often are you following up with the person to get a response?

We tend to do things for people we have positive relationships with and put others on the backburner. Not getting responses is a good indicator that it's time to analyze your relationship.

Q: How do I respond to a senior director who places a last minute request/demand on me that will require me to stay until 9 p.m.?

A: In our careers, hard work and dedication are rewarded. That does not mean that you have to stay late every night, but there will be times where the extra hours are necessary to stay ahead of the game. That being said, the best way to respond to any demand is with honesty. If you are willing to stay and get it done, state your intentions. If you have previously scheduled dinner plans to celebrate a friend's birthday or just need to unplug, state you are unable to stay and be clear on when you will be able to complete the request.

Every company and manager has different expectations when it comes to staying late and putting in extra hours. If the culture does not fit with your mindset, it is best to have a transparent conversation with your boss. If your boss doesn't agree with your mindset, you may never be truly successful within that culture. If you are the boss, keep in mind that no two people are the same in their workflow.

Circumstances create boundaries. Both the employee and the boss set the boundaries. These are necessary discussions and they need to be transparent. If someone will invest the time, and the work always gets done but on a different schedule, it is probably not a battle to fight. Appreciate your colleague for her investment, whether it's on your schedule or not, as long as demands are met.

Keep in mind that showing ambition, ability, knowledge, and a pattern of achievement will ultimately provide you with leverage to set boundaries with your colleagues and your boss.

Q: If I met someone at a company meeting more than six months ago, is it appropriate for me to ask him or her to repeat his or her name?

A: Yes, it is appropriate to state that you haven't seen each other since that last company meeting and your memory is failing you. It is also appropriate to ask a peer for a quick refresher on names, if possible. If you have been introduced to that person more than two times, it is not a good idea to ask the person to remind you of his or her name. It makes it seem as though you have no real interest in that person. Human nature dictates, "If you don't have an interest in me, I don't have an interest in you." When you do remember names, it sets you apart, and people will be more interested in you. It is a relationship builder.

Q: How do you handle a coworker who misses project deadlines that affect you or your team?

A: The best way to handle this situation is to meet with the coworker individually. Before you meet with him or her, think about what drives that person. What is his or her agenda? Is something causing this behavior?

Seek to understand what is actually happening. Here are some good statements and questions to discuss with your colleague:

> "I'd like to share my concerns about the project and the deadlines."

> "May we take a few moments to reflect and discuss what was agreed on in the past regarding this and other projects and our deadlines?"

> ≫ "Do you know the challenge we face when the deadline is missed?"

> ≫ "What will it take to ensure the deadlines are met?"

> ≫ "What do you think the solution may be for us to be more collaborative and get the work done in a timely manner?"

If you have had a professional conversation with this person, made agreements, and set a solution, you are on your way to a successful project. If you decide to take the passive-aggressive route and talk about the person behind his or her back but don't say anything to him or her directly, the likelihood of a long-term solution is little to none.

Q: Do you have to accept LinkedIn requests from work/professional colleagues?

A: LinkedIn is a way to keep up with your colleagues and their companies. There is no reason not to connect with someone in a professional manner when you know him or her professionally. If you do not know the person but he is requesting to connect with you, look to see with whom he is connected. If you have a mutual colleague, accept. Again, there is no reason not to connect. The only time it is better not to connect is when you see the person is not credible. For instance, I had someone who wanted to connect with me who did not seem to have a profession or any information on her LinkedIn page. I chose not to connect.

Q: Do you have to accept Facebook or other personal social media requests from people you work with? What if I want to keep my personal business private? Many of my colleagues send me Facebook requests and I'm not sure what to do.

A: Not only do you not have to accept requests from professional affiliations, but in most cases you should not. There should be a line, albeit a fine one at times, between your personal life and professional life. By drawing that line, you are not inauthentic. The most professional and successful people do not bring 100 percent of their personal lives into work. Although they do blend, they do not need to completely overlap. Everyone has situations in their personal life that challenge them. There is no reason that your professional colleagues need to know about all of those challenges.

The other point we would like to note is that you have no control over what your friends post. Personally, I don't think I would always want my professional colleagues to see the comments or posts from friends, or friends of friends. While they may be fun or funny, they do not contribute to my professional brand.

Make sure that your privacy settings are set correctly. A client of ours just told a story about a person who had an inappropriate photograph of himself at a party that anyone on Facebook could see, not just his friends. That person did not get hired because of the photograph.

Q: Is it acceptable to eat in meetings?

A: I went to a meeting last week with a client and one of the people sitting in the meeting took out a bag of chips and proceeded to eat. The other meeting participants were obviously distracted. You could see people's eyes darting to her every time she crunched on a chip. While this is not the worst thing that could happen, why would anyone reduce their impact in a meeting because they were hungry? Our answer to this question is, no, it is not acceptable to eat in meetings where no one else is eating.

Q: What if I sent an email and unintentionally threw someone under the bus?

A: First things first: Do the right thing whether the person was copied or not, or whether she knows yet or not. Go directly to that person and apologize, face to face when possible. Be prepared to state the facts of the given situation and what happened. Always apologize and accept responsibility. Not taking responsibility and not being accountable will burn a bridge in a fast and furious way. Also, let the person know how much you value the relationship.

After you have done that, go to the person or people you sent the message to and set the story straight.

Chapter 18

You Are Your Competitive Advantage

If you don't have a competitive advantage, don't compete.

—Jack Welch

Some of the situations you just read about may seem minor or obvious. Remember what bothers you about working with others and how that has affected the overall interaction or longevity of the relationship. If at any point in your career someone looked at you and thought, He did that?! or She did that?! you have decreased your chances of success. Each day gives you an opportunity to make the day work to your advantage. As Stephen Covey says, "Begin with the end in mind." Each morning, ask yourself where you want to be in your career. Make sure everything you do that day supports your goal. Don't allow things that could be prevented to get in your way.

Challenge yourself daily to exceed all expectations. Remember that you can be whoever you set your mind to be and do whatever you set out to do. If you stay focused, you will become a true professional.

Your opportunities for growth in business are endless if your technical and people skills are fine-tuned. As we mentioned, luck is when opportunity meets preparedness. Keep this in mind as you begin each day. You—and *only* you— are in charge of how lucky you will be. Your skills for managing situations successfully, with confidence and absolute clarity, can be powerful tools. If you fail to invest in yourself, you fail the preparedness part of the equation.

When it comes to competition, we can agree that not everyone wins. It is important to reflect on your past failures and learn from them. If you want to get better, you must do some root-cause analysis to uncover what you can change to improve next time. If you are being passed over for a promotion, not receiving an opportunity for a second interview, or not being assigned the quality of work you believe you are capable of, then find out why.

As you encounter others in all business situations, take note of what works and what doesn't work in terms of influence and impact. So often the lessons we need to learn to set us apart can be witnessed daily. If you are aware of your surroundings and have specific goals to help develop your professionalism, you will find lessons in action. Each day, thoughts, habits, and priorities you chose, both good and bad, will determine your results. Take time to plan the possibilities, and then execute in the moment.

Another way to stay ahead of your competition is to do your research. Invest time and money in magazines, books, news sources, blogs, and conversations. Ask questions, search for topics and content, and process what you learn. So often, people research like crazy to obtain a job, yet fail to continue the research to get the next job. Set yourself apart and contribute interesting statistics and content in an effort to impact your business. If you are prepared for every business circumstance, you will find that, indeed, you are your competitive advantage!

Chapter 19 > Your Action Plan for Continued Success

Any idea is useless unless put into action. We have found that many of the professionals we work with are excellent at the large-scale, impactful aspects of their positions but do not take care of their overall reputations. They do not know how to put a book like this into action.

Here is a specific action plan to keep you on track:

1. Write down one to three specific career goals you have at the moment. For instance, a promotion, a sales goal, a client relationship goal, or a collaboration goal.

2. Write down the key stakeholders who are relevant to your specific goal and what their hot buttons are regarding what they expect from you. For example:

Goal:

My goal is to be perceived as an important contributor in meetings with my colleagues and boss.

Stakeholders' hot buttons:

John: Timeliness
Sundar: Error-free work

Beth: Concise written material

Dee: Confident demeanor, know what you're
           talking about when you speak up in a meeting

Francois: Presents well, put together well

3. Go through each chapter with three highlighters:
One color signifies what you need to *start* doing, as
it will make a difference in your career; the second
color signifies what you need to *continue* doing and
may not do consistently; and the third color signifies what you need to *stop* doing, the actions that are
stalling or stopping your career growth.

Start: Arriving at meetings five minutes early or
          letting the meeting organizer know that I
          will be five minutes late.

Continue: Putting away my telephone or not looking at
          my computer when others are talking to me.
          Speaking up with confidence, not arrogance,
          in meetings.

Stop: Writing emotional emails; put anything I am
          not sure about into my drafts to review an
          hour later.

4. With those expectations in mind, take three points
from each highlighted color in each chapter and create your action plan.

The Chapter Checklist, Metrics Measuring

Below is a list of goals and successful strategies—the
opposite of each big blunder we have described. Go through
this checklist on a weekly basis. How will you measure your
success? Define your performance metrics and follow them
monthly. Modify when necessary. These are examples to set

up specific behavior metrics in each chapter. Take the time to tailor this list to yourself. Each chapter could have many behaviors to support your goal.

1. **Staying One Step Ahead**
   ✓ Goal: Keep my emotions in check.
   ✓ I kept my emotions in check during weekly meetings and stopped raising my voice.

2. **Using Body Language Properly**
   ✓ Goal: Smile more; everyone says that I look angry.
   ✓ I smiled throughout the day to build rapport. I especially focused on this while walking through the hallways instead of keeping my head down.

3. **Professional Written and Verbal Correspondence**
   ✓ Goal: Go out of my way to thank people for helping me; do not just expect it.
   ✓ I sent two thank-you notes to my colleagues who went out of their way to help me on a couple of projects.

4. **Following the Rules for Introductions**
   ✓ Goal: Remember to introduce and reintroduce myself, even if it feels uncomfortable.
   ✓ I reintroduced myself in meetings this week to people I do not see on a regular basis.

5. **Making Small Talk and Networking Appropriately**
   ✓ Goal: Find out more about my colleagues and don't talk as much about myself.
   ✓ I was interested, not interesting. I asked three questions before I shared information about myself, and then kept bringing it back to them.

6. Remembering Names

✓ Goal: Remember the names of people I am introduced to and use their names throughout the conversation.

✓ I was conscious of not thinking about what I was going to say, and stopped to focus on the person's name when he introduced himself. I was able to remember four people's names this week.

7. Using Technology Etiquette

✓ Goal: Send professional emails. My boss has commented on three occasions about typos and about the inappropriate emotion in my emails.

✓ I reread every email this week to make sure there were no typos and also to make sure that they weren't emotionally charged.

8. Cubicle Professionalism and Guidelines

✓ Goal: Don't put all my "stuff" up in my cubicle. The president of the company made a joke about my workspace at the last meeting and it made me aware that she didn't think it was very professional. I wondered if she felt I was not as competent as I am because of it.

✓ I did not hang up all of my Mardi Gras beads, only a few strands.

9. Following the Guidelines for Professional Dress

✓ Goal: Dress more professionally. I have noticed that everyone around me looks more professional, and I realize they really do command more respect in meetings.

✓ I wore a suit to a meeting where some people were in business casual and others were in business attire. I was conscious of the message I wanted to send about my brand.

10. Using Meeting Etiquette

✓ Goal: Don't hold sidebar conversations during meetings. I heard that Allen was annoyed that I was not engaged in his meeting last week because Erin and I were having a conversation. Even though it was on topic, I realize that Allen thought it was unprofessional and affected his message.

✓ I listened during the meeting on Wednesday and did not hold the sidebar conversation I wanted to have with Trudy.

11. Being Prepared for Interviews

✓ Goal: Be prepared for my interviews. Last week when the interviewer asked if I had any questions about the company, I realized I had not done enough research about who they were, over and above what they actually did.

✓ I did my homework on the company I interviewed with this week, so I had three specific questions about their values in the marketplace.

12. Using Professional Telephone Etiquette and Protocol

✓ Goal: Stay focused during calls. I realize that I am missing important information because I am catching up on emails during the weekly status call.

✓ I did not multitask when I was on the Monday morning department status call.

13. Choosing the Appropriate Gift

✓ Goal: Buy appropriate gifts for my colleagues and clients for special occasions and holidays. I bought a bottle of wine for a client and was told by his assistant that he didn't drink and that vendors are not allowed to give gifts to them.

✓ I proactively took the time to think about the appropriate gift for my client Sally. After doing some research, I found out she only likes red wine and chose an appropriate bottle.

14. Professionalism While Traveling

✓ Goal: think about my brand while actually traveling, not only at the meetings I attend. The gentleman on the plane next to me looked so professional, and when we were discussing our jobs, I felt very sloppy. I wished that I had chosen to wear something that represented my company better. I hate apologizing for how I look.

✓ I took the time to think about what I was wearing on the plane to my business meeting on Tuesday. I felt as though I represented my brand and my company well.

15. Global Awareness and Maturity

✓ Goal: Be more aware of the cultural protocol of my company. Now that I am traveling internationally, I realized that I do not know how to handle myself properly when out of my country. It makes me and others uncomfortable.

✓ I found out that business card protocol is important to my Asian client and handled it exactly as the guide told me when I met with him.

16. The Professional Intern

✓ Goal: Make the most of my internship. When they interviewed me, they said I would be doing a lot more than I am doing, and it is annoying and feels like a waste of my summer. This is not what I thought it would be, but I know there is something to learn and I need to apply myself.

✓ I arrived early to work and went straight to my manager to find out what more I could be doing for them and let her know that I have time to help with more projects.

17. Handling Sticky Situations

✓ Goal: Not assuming the reason behind others' actions. I have a terrible habit of thinking the worst when something occurs at work. Sometimes I feel as though people do not respect me as much as I deserve, but I know thinking this way is not helping my career.

✓ I did not react when I found out that I had not been included in an important meeting on Thursday. I took the time to find out what happened by having a calm and professional conversation with Hubert.

18. You Are Your Competitive Advantage

✓ Goal: Be more purposeful regarding my career. Sometimes I think of things I should be doing to help me achieve my goals within my company, but then I do not write them down. I seem to forget until something comes up the next time.

✓ I wrote down three things that would give me a competitive advantage and I looked at them every day this week.

19. Your Action Plan for Continued Success

✓ Goal: Take the time to sharpen my professional saw. I am always so busy with my day-to-day tasks and my personal life that I do not take time out to breathe and plan my career purposefully.

✓ I scheduled 30 minutes on Friday to go through my checklist and see if I had met my goals from last week and if I needed to revise them for the following week.

Print this out to create your own metric checklist:

1. Staying One Step Ahead

2. Using Body Language Properly

3. Professional Written and Verbal Correspondence

4. Following the Rules for Introductions

5. Making Small Talk and Networking Appropriately

6. Remembering Names

7. Using Technology Etiquette

8. Cubicle Professionalism and Guidelines

9. Following the Guidelines for Professional Dress

10. Using Meeting Etiquette

11. Being Prepared for Interviews

12. Using Professional Telephone Etiquette and Protocol

13. Choosing the Appropriate Gift

14. Professionalism while Traveling

15. Global Awareness and Maturity

16. The Professional Intern

17. Handling Sticky Situations

18. You Are Your Competitive Advantage

19. Your Action Plan for Continued Success

⟩Notes

Chapter 2

1. "Amy J. C. Cuddy," faculty profile at Harvard Business School. Online at *http://www.hbs.edu/faculty/Pages/profile.aspx?facId=491042*.

2. Greg L. Stewart, Susan L. Dustin, Murray R. Barrick, and Todd C. Darnold, *Journal of Applied Psychology* 93(5): September 2008, 1139–46. Online at *http://dx.doi.org/10.1037/0021-9010.93.5.1139*.

3. Julia Layton, "Does Smiling Make You Happy?" Online at *https://createhappinesswithyou.wordpress.com/2010/11/07/does-smiling-make-you-happy-by-julia-layton*.

Daniel Goleman, "A Feel-Good Theory: A Smile Affects Mood," *New York Times*, July 18, 1989. Online at *http://www.nytimes.com/1989/07/18/science/a-feel-good-theory-a-smile-affects-mood.html*.

Chapter 7

1. "UT Arlington Study Shows Employees Become Angry When Receiving After-Hours Electronic Correspondence," University of Texas–Arlington. Online at *https://www.uta.edu/news/releases/2015/02/butts-afterhour-communications.php*.

Chapter 9

1. Adapted from "Business Professional versus Business Casual: Who Wins the Fight in Sales?" *PJF Training Blog*, March 13, 2013. Online at *http://pjftraining.com/blog/business-professional-versus-business-casual-who-wins-the-fight-in-sales*.

2. Andy Yates, "Should You Still Dress to Impress at Work?" KeltonGlobal.com, October 3, 2014. Online at *http://keltonglobal.com/in-the-media/should-you-still-dress-to-impress-at-work*.

3. "Your Lack of Mascara Is a Sign of Your Utter Incompetence (re: Cosmetics as a Feature of the Extended Human Phenotype: Modulation of the Perception of Biologically Important Facial Signals)." Online at *http://regender.org/news-center/in-the-news/your-lack-mascara-sign-your-utter-incompetence-re-cosmetics-feature-extended*.

Nancy L. Etcoff, Shannon Stock, Lauren E. Haley, Sarah A. Vickery, and David House,

"Cosmetics as a Feature of the Extended Human Phenotype: Modulation of the Perception of Biologically Important Facial Signals," *PLOS ONE* 6(10): October 3, 2011. Online at *doi:10.1371/journal.pone.0025656*.

4. "Making the Case Against Business Casual," *Inside Business*, January 8, 2010. Online at *http://www.theimagearchitect.com/press_articles/making-case-against-business-casual.htm*.

Chapter 19

1. University of Sheffield in London. Online at *https://www.sheffield.ac.uk/careers/students/advice/intercultural*.

Index

About the Authors

KIM ZOLLER and **KERRY PRESTON** are recognized experts in leadership development. For more than two decades, their focus has been on personal and professional development in the C-suite, as well as on all levels of individuals and teams within organizations. They lead Image Dynamics, an innovative professional development firm that collaborates with companies to develop their people and processes by providing results-oriented training solutions, customized training programs, advanced executive coaching, customer surveys, and long-term strategic development.

Kim and Kerry believe that training is only useful when there is direct application to business outcomes. Their goal is to provide their clients with the knowledge and ability to apply the training tools they deliver.

Both Kim and Kerry are dynamic international speakers who assist individuals and companies with the necessary tools to be successful in today's competitive market. Kim, Kerry, and their team have trained more than 100,000 individuals since 1992.

JAICO PUBLISHING HOUSE
Elevate Your Life. Transform Your World.

ESTABLISHED IN 1946, Jaico Publishing House is home to world-transforming authors such as Sri Sri Paramahansa Yogananda, Osho, The Dalai Lama, Sri Sri Ravi Shankar, Sadhguru, Robin Sharma, Deepak Chopra, Jack Canfield, Eknath Easwaran, Devdutt Pattanaik, Khushwant Singh, John Maxwell, Brian Tracy and Stephen Hawking.

Our late founder Mr. Jaman Shah first established Jaico as a book distribution company. Sensing that independence was around the corner, he aptly named his company Jaico ('Jai' means victory in Hindi). In order to service the significant demand for affordable books in a developing nation, Mr. Shah initiated Jaico's own publications. Jaico was India's first publisher of paperback books in the English language.

While self-help, religion and philosophy, mind/body/spirit, and business titles form the cornerstone of our non-fiction list, we publish an exciting range of travel, current affairs, biography, and popular science books as well. Our renewed focus on popular fiction is evident in our new titles by a host of fresh young talent from India and abroad. Jaico's recently established Translations Division translates selected English content into nine regional languages.

Jaico's Higher Education Division (HED) is recognized for its student-friendly textbooks in Business Management and Engineering which are in use countrywide.

In addition to being a publisher and distributor of its own titles, Jaico is a major national distributor of books of leading international and Indian publishers. With its headquarters in Mumbai, Jaico has branches and sales offices in Ahmedabad, Bangalore, Bhopal, Bhubaneswar, Chennai, Delhi, Hyderabad, Kolkata and Lucknow.

SINCE 1946